The Whiskies of Scotland

This is a new enlarged edition of Dr. McDowall's most successful account of whisky, both blended and malts, with the historical background of the distilleries of Scotland.

Since the uisguebeatha drunk by the hardy Gaels meant 'water of life', it is not altogether surprising that, in an attempt to control the production of whisky, supervision of its manufacture was put in the hands of the Royal College of Surgeons in Edinburgh in 1505. In England, under King Charles the First, the Worshipful Company of Distillers was formed by doctors for the same purpose. Grain unfit for human consumption was commonly used and it became essential to ensure that the 'water of life' was non-toxic. Nowadays most connoisseurs dispense with the water.

THE WHISKIES OF SCOTLAND

R. J. S. McDowall

M.D., D.Sc.

Professor Emeritus, University of London

JOHN MURRAY

First published 1967
Reprinted 1968
Second edition 1971
Third edition (with Supplement) 1975

Printed in Great Britain by
REDWOOD BURN LIMITED
Trowbridge & Esher
0 7195 3211 6

Contents

Contents

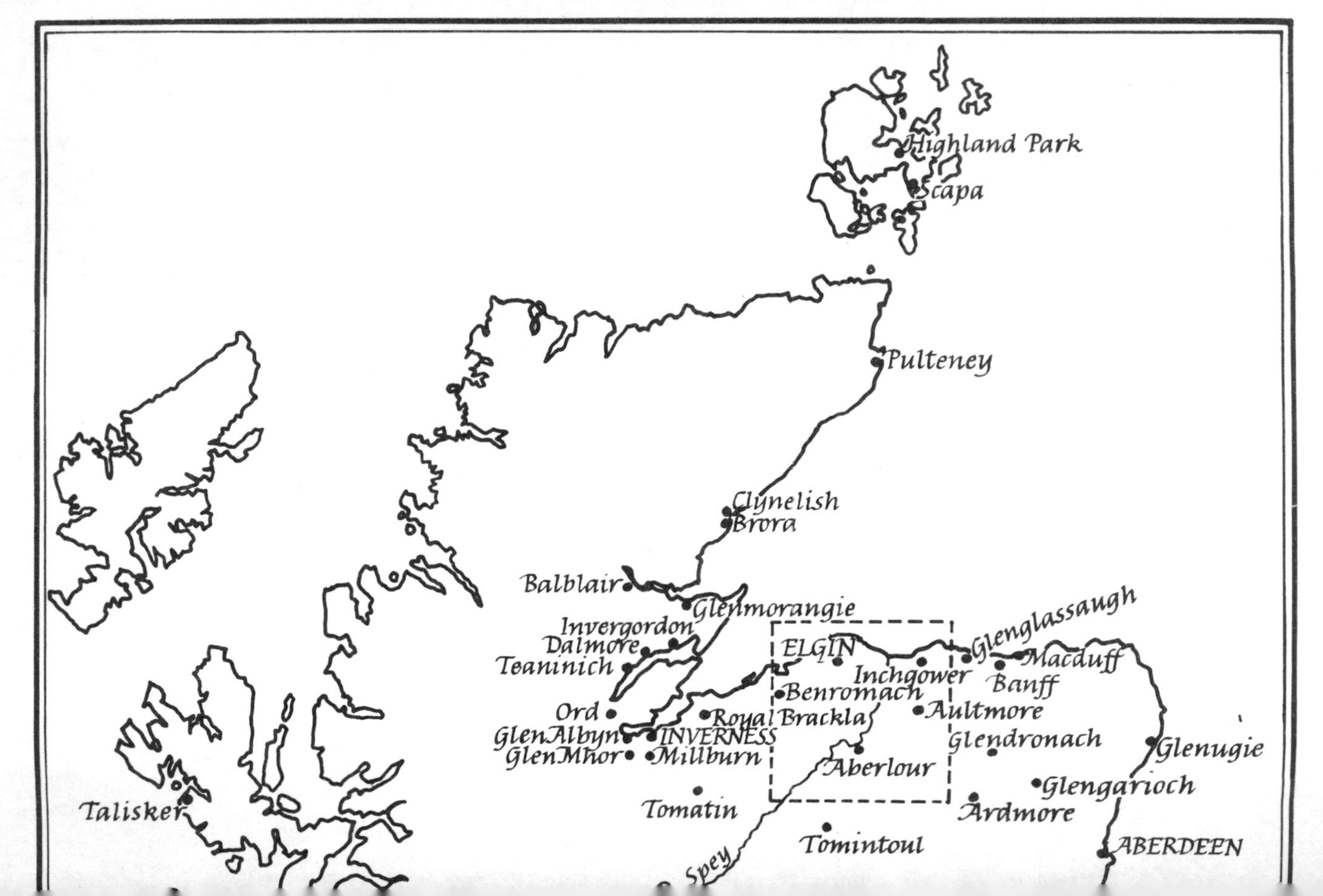
Highland Park
Scapa
Pulteney
Clynelish
Brora
Balblair
Glenmorangie
Invergordon
Dalmore
Teaninich
Ord
Glen Albyn
Glen Mhor
INVERNESS
Millburn
Royal Brackla
Tomatin
ELGIN
Benromach
Inchgower
Aultmore
Aberlour
Tomintoul
Spey
Glenglassaugh
Macduff
Banff
Glendronach
Glenugie
Glengarioch
Ardmore
ABERDEEN
Talisker

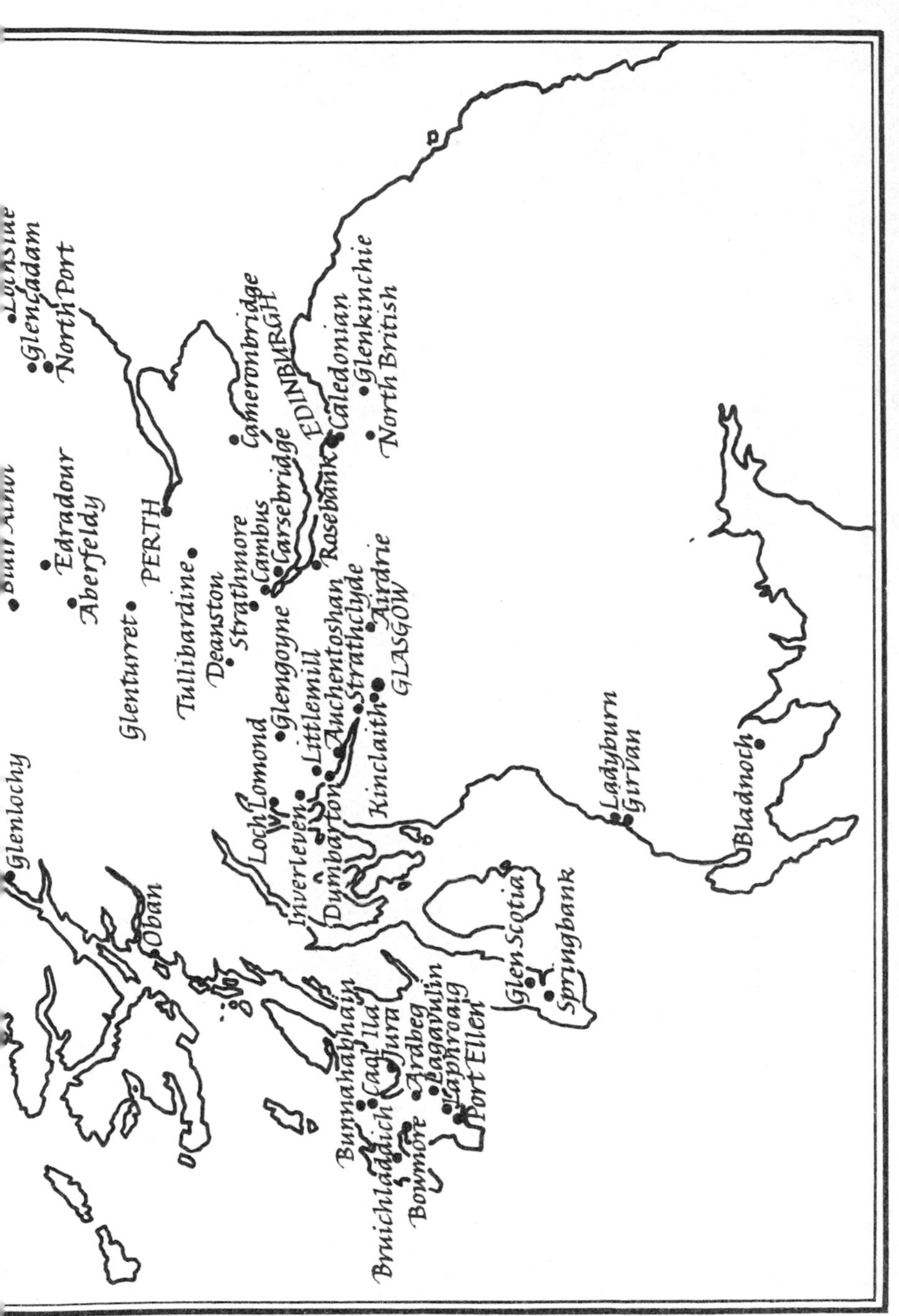

Scotland: showing the main distilleries

For details of area in dotted square see p.13

Preface to the First Edition

The world has begun to drink whisky in a large way, but it is quite remarkable how little has been written about it. Whiskies are almost as numerous and varied as the wines of France, but there is no general account from which their story can be easily gleaned.

This book is written to supply the need. In its preparation I have visited all the malt distilleries of which single malt whiskies are available on the retail market and have collected samples of each (alas not free samples!). My information is therefore first hand and can readily be confirmed. In forming opinions I have had the advice of many of my knowledgeable and discerning friends from the Hampstead Golf Club.

It has been a very pleasant task visiting distilleries over a period of years, for they are usually situated in very pleasant and often quite remote places, while the distillers are a very agreeable, contented people who are always happy to share their knowledge with others.

It has obviously not been possible to collect all the blends for there are too many, indeed there are many registered blends of which only the names exist. I have had, therefore, to content myself with describing those of the larger blending houses which I know, but I am sure there are many good blends which I have yet to experience. In compiling this book I owe much to the many companies who have supplied me with information and checked my writing, to the distillery managers who have shown me round the distilleries, and especially to my wife who has visited them with me and helped in the preparation.

Preface to the Second Edition

The demand for a new edition of this book, especially after a reprint and four foreign editions, Swedish, German, Spanish and American, suggests that it has fulfilled what it set out to do, to give for the first time a simple general account of the subject.

Its success has also given its sober publisher a new view of its future. It has also made possible a complete resetting with a larger page size, a very extensive revision, many additions, new maps and a new illustration of a Coffey Still to which blended whisky owes more than it generally admits!

Since this book was published in 1967, three others have appeared, showing the growing interest in whisky. They overlap remarkably little and are for the most part more literary and complementary to the present work, which appears to be taking a permanent place in establishing a factual knowledge of the subject.

It is of interest too that, as a distiller has written to me: 'There is no doubt, in our view, that discerning members of the public are becoming interested in and aware of malt whisky and although we would never expect to talk in terms of the sort of figures that interest the big blenders, we certainly see malt whisky taking a reasonable share of the premium market'. This has been confirmed by many retailers.

For the figures of the consumption of whisky I am indebted to the well-known authority, Mr William Birnie of Glenmhor fame, and for the diagram of the Coffey Still to McMillan of Edinburgh, the greatest maker of stills in Scotland.

Once more I am grateful to a number of distinguished and knowledgeable friends—moderate drinkers who like a free drink but prefer to remain anonymous.

Introduction

The origin of whisky is hidden in the mists of antiquity. Wine made from barley was certainly known to the ancient Greeks. Some think it came, like Christianity, to Scotland from Ireland. This may or may not be so, but certainly it was the domestic drink of the Highlands of Scotland from very early times. It was distilled for the households of the chiefs and their friends as brandy is to-day in France.

Its name is derived from the Gaelic uisge-beatha, sometimes written Usqua, or shortened to Usky, meaning the water of life —an obvious relation of the *aqua vitae* of many countries, but of a very different character.

Whisky had already reached the Court of King James the Fourth by the year 1500. It is recorded in the Scottish Exchequer Roll of 1494–5 that eight bolls of malt were given to Friar John Cor to make *aqua vitae*. The well-known chronicler Hollinshed extolled the virtues of whisky as early as 1577 as follows: (Beying moderately taken, sayeth he, it cutteth fleume, it lighteneth the mynd, it quickeneth the spirits, it cureth the hydropsie, it healeth the stranguary, it pounceth the stone, it repelleth gravel, it puffeth away ventositie, it kepyth and preserveth the hed from whyrlying, the eyes from dazelying, the tongue from lispying, the mouthe from snafflying, the teethe from chatterying, the throte from rattlying, the weasan from stieflying, the stomach from womblying, the harte from swellyng, the bellie from wirtching, the guts from rumblying, the hands from shivering, the sinoews from shrinkyng, the veynes from crumplyng, the bones from akying, the marrow from soakyng, and truly it is a sovereign liquor if it be ordlie taken.) A bit enthusiastic perhaps but approximately true. In Edinburgh distilling was such a popular and lucrative pastime that some attempt was made to control it in 1505 by placing supervision of its manufacture in the hands of the newly formed Royal

College of Surgeons of the City. In London, The Worshipful Company of Distillers was formed by doctors for a similar purpose in the reign of Charles the First. Prior to that time cereals unfit for human consumption were in common use; indeed, it would seem that the making of alcohol was a common method of utilising cereals which had fermented as a result of wet harvests when the grain could not be dried. The Scots have always abhorred waste. Some of the whisky must indeed have been very rough and toxic stuff. Even to-day men working at silos, now in common use in farms, sometimes become seriously ill from drinking the alcoholic effluent from fermented cereals.

The distilling process, which simply consists of driving off the flavoured alcohol by heat and subsequently condensing the vapour, does much to reduce its toxicity. The apparatus needed for the making of small quantities was relatively small and easily concealed, a fact which made illicit stills very difficult to control. Whisky distilling was not really controlled till the Highlands of Scotland were subdued as never before after the rebellion of Prince Charles in 1745. Satisfactory legislation and taxation was introduced in 1823 and led to the almost total disappearance of the illicit stills which had been so prevalent. The taxation was negligible and very different from the £2·20 a bottle of to-day!

In Scotland, whisky has long been and still is the drink of the occasion. It is used to celebrate births and marriages, and at funerals the chief mourner has a duty to regale those who have attended. There is commonly an inn at the cemetery gate.

In England the advent of whisky was slower. For the most part the English drank ale and beer. When William and Mary came to England in 1688 the drinking of gin became the mode as a compliment to royalty. The making of gin, which previously came from Holland, was then encouraged.

Modern gin is really a very close relation to whisky, being simply a grain spirit similar to that used in the blending of whisky, but the spirit is further purified by additional distillation, usually in a pot still with flavouring agents added, especially coriander and juniper (genevre) from which it gets its name.

By the time of the early Georges, gin became so cheap and popular and its use became such a scandal that it had to be prohibited. Prohibition, as ever, was a failure and increased taxation took its place. Gin lost face and became popularly known as 'Mother's Ruin', strikingly portrayed by Hogarth's 'Gin Lane', and as late as 1920 Professor Saintsbury referred to 'that humble and much reviled liquid which is the most specially English of all spirits'.

Until the middle of the nineteenth century the whisky drunk in England was the milder Lowland variety, and that in small quantity, but the whole outlook changed with the invention of the patent still in 1830 and the introduction of blending a little later. Blended whisky (see page 51) was introduced to London by five great companies, John Dewar, James Buchanan (Black and White), James Mackie (White Horse), soon to be followed by John Walker and John Haig, who had already established themselves in Scotland. The blended whiskies were not so heavy as the old Highland malts and were found more suited to the sedentary life of the townsman. Modern malts are, however, better made and are not so heavy.

The introduction of whisky was no doubt greatly aided by the disease of the vines in France and Spain which led to a great shortage of wine and brandy, which were till then the drinks of the well-to-do. Sir Winston Churchill has recorded that the drink of his father was brandy and soda, a drink which is now quite uncommon. Whisky has taken the place of the brandy.

In the 1920's gin made a social comeback in the form of the cocktail introduced from America as an aperitif before dinner, but slowly it has become replaced by whisky, especially on the Continent and in the United States. In the latter, where good sherry has always been scarce, a guest is expected to drink whisky as an aperitif in various guises: whisky 'on the rocks' (neat on ice), whisky 'sour' (with lemon), or 'old fashioned' (with angostura, soda and fruit), all of which completely ruin the flavour of good whisky. Whisky may also be drunk at a cocktail party, but it is not so usual to drink whisky later in the evening, as is done in this country. In France to-day, whisky plain, with soda or with ice, is the mode as an aperitif. This no doubt is responsible for the enormous increase in whisky consumption in that country in the last ten years.

All this, together with the repeal of prohibition in America, has led to an enormous growth in the whisky industry which is now having its greatest boom ever.

It is on record that in 1945 Winston Churchill minuted for the Ministry of Food 'On no account reduce the amount of barley for whisky. It takes years to mature and is an invaluable export and dollar earner. Having regard to our difficulties about export, it would be improvident not to preserve this characteristic element of British ascendancy.' During the war the distilleries had done good work by making yeast for bread, alcohol to replace petrol, and acetone used in the manufacture of explosives, but cereals became in such short supply that many of the smaller distilleries had to close down.

The American whiskies, although not all unpleasant to drink, like the old Highland malts tend in my experience to be heavier and have more after-effects than Scotch, for which there is now a demand limited only by its availability and its price. The great sale of the blends has led to a greater demand for malt whisky, indeed so much so that many disused distilleries have been reconditioned and brought back into production, while so many single malt whiskies now go for blending that only one-half of those made are available as such. Their excellence must, however, never be lost sight of. They are as varied as the wines and as delicious to those who know how to choose. The heart of any good blended whisky is a good malt whisky.

SCOTCH TO-DAY

So we come to 'Scotch' to-day. Everything which comes from Scotland, its tartans, its bagpipes and its lassies, is Scottish but its whisky is 'Scotch'. Ask for a large Scotch and you get whisky.

Scotch whisky to-day has become a very standardised product, made under very careful and skilled supervision, of the best possible ingredients. Three varieties are clearly recognised—malt whisky, grain whisky and blended whisky.

Malt whisky is made entirely from a watery extract of malted barley (see page 101), fermented by yeast and distilled in what are almost standard onion-shaped pot stills from which the flavoured alcohol is driven off by heat. Malt whisky takes from ten to fifteen years to mature properly but alas may be sold after three years.

Grain whisky is made mostly from maize, almost entirely imported, the starch of the mashed maize being broken down to maltose by adding a small quantity of malted barley. It is fermented by yeast, but it is distilled in a Coffey or patent still in which the alcohol is driven off by steam. This is a purer whisky than malt in the sense that it is nearer pure alcohol, but it has therefore appreciably less flavour than malt whisky and does not take so long to mature. It is also much cheaper to make, but this is masked by taxation based on its alcoholic content.

Blended whisky is a mixture of malt and grain whiskies, in the best blends in almost equal parts, thus securing the purity of the grain with the flavour of the malt. This is the whisky most generally available, but its quality depends on the malts it contains. Alas, many blends, some with fancy names and in fancy bottles, contain a much higher proportion of grain whisky disguised by peat. In all fairness it must however be said that grain whisky, if taken in moderation, is quite harmless.

Wi' tippeny [ale] we fear nae evil
Wi' usquebae, we'll face the devil.

BURNS

I. The Malt Whiskies

For the most part the malt whiskies come from the Highlands of Scotland, north of Perth, lands of hills and valleys, of lochs and mountain streams, of much poor land but of very good water. The barley from which they are made came originally from the coastal strips which surround the central highlands and from a few of the beautiful valleys, but now much is imported from the Lothians, Lincolnshire and East Anglia.

One river is specially associated with whisky making, the River Spey, which gives its name to the elegant Highland dance the Strathspey. If you arrive from the south you probably first notice the river as a small stream just as it leaves its remote mountain origins between the Caledonian Canal and the road to Inverness between Dalnaspidal and Newtonmore. Now it winds its way northwards, first through bare hill lands, then through picturesque valleys and woodlands till it reaches the rich northern plain to open into the Moray Firth at Speymouth some 10 miles north-east of Elgin. A good road accompanies it and we pass such holiday resorts as Kingussie, Aviemore and on to Grantown-on-Spey where it is best to cross to the east bank of the river. Between here and Elgin, a distance of only 33 miles, there are no fewer than 28 distilleries all within a mile or so of the road. Strathspey is indeed the centre of the whisky industry. (See maps.)

The laich or lowlands north of the Grampians, sometimes called the garden of Scotland, enjoys a most equable climate, due it is said to the sweep of the Gulf Stream round the north of Scotland. Its gardens with rich soil four or six feet deep, swept down from the Grampians through centuries, are a joy to horticulturists.

The Spey is famous for its salmon and for being the fastest-flowing river in Britain, but most of all it is famous for its whisky. There are more distilleries along the valley of the Spey and its tributaries than anywhere else in the world. Now, however, it must be remarked that very few of the distilleries actually draw their water supply from the Spey. They get it from adjacent wells and rivulets, indeed, the Spey is the main drain of the distilleries. Well may we ask why this occurs. First and foremost the area immediately north of the Grampians has a good rainfall, peat is easily available and the coastal plain is extremely rich and suitable for growing barley. Actually to-day barley richer in starch is commonly imported and nowadays much peat comes from Aberdeenshire. Besides, and this was very important before the days of good roads and motor cars, the region of the Spey was conveniently removed from the excisemen and illicit stills abounded. Men knew from birth how to make whisky, or as the Duke of Gordon told the House of Lords in 1822, the Highlanders were born distillers.

At Craigellachie we can recross the Spey and, leaving it on the right, proceed by the main road north to Rothes, passing a whole series of distilleries till we reach Elgin. With the exception of the famous Glen Grant Distilleries at Rothes, the distilleries are all relatively small and similar, making excellent whisky, most of which goes to the blenders.

Elgin is, indeed, a charming county town of great character with the remains of what must have been a very beautiful cathedral, built in the thirteenth century, standing in extensive well-kept precints, adjoining a large public park. There are also many beautiful Georgian houses. The cathedral was destroyed as long ago as 1390, by the notorious Wolf of Badenoch, Earl of Buchan, a son of King Robert the second, to avenge his excommunication by the local Bishop of Murray. The king did, however, make his son do penance at the Cross which is still to be seen in the High Street.

Elgin may be described as the whisky capital of Scotland. All roads to and from it abound with distilleries and the whole of the surrounding area has rich fields of barley. In the town, too, is the imposing new headquarters of the Scottish Malt Distillers, which controls malt whisky production for the great Distillers Company. Elgin is also a centre for the bottling of the Spey whiskies, notably by the firms of Gordon & McPhail and Campbell, Hope & King, both of outstanding reliability.

As the maps show, the area between the rivers Deveron and Findhorn includes the most of the malt distilleries in Scotland, although there are a few on the coastal fringe to the east and north as far as Wick. Then in the west we have surprisingly seven distilleries on the island of Islay, one on the little island of Jura, one in Skye, two at Campbeltown, one on Mull, one at Oban and two at Fort William.

Malt whisky is, as has been said, the original whisky and is wholly distilled from fermented extract of malted barley and matured in oak casks, preferably those which have been recently used for the import of sherry. The actual process is given in more detail in a later chapter. This all sounds simple and theoretically could be done in any country, yet after hundreds of years of whisky making only the distilleries of Scotland and Ireland have survived. (Irish whiskey—note the 'e' in the spelling—is quite a distinct product from 'Scotch'.) Many other countries now try to make whisky.

The whisky trade has long distinguished four varieties of Scottish malts—Highland, Lowland, Islay and Campbeltown. The Islay malts have the strongest flavour, the Highland malts the most subtle, but the Lowland and Campbeltown malts are milder and now very much alike. Their differentiation probably had its origin when there were very many distilleries in Campbeltown producing a strongly flavoured whisky.

There are about 110 malt distilleries in operation, but more are under construction. Less than 30 of their whiskies are available to the public in bottle. Most are wholly taken by the blenders and now there are over two thousand registered blends; indeed, when most people talk of whisky they refer to a blend. The single malt whiskies are not always easily available and are a few shillings more expensive than standard blends because of the longer time needed for them to mature. Like the blends they are commonly available at 70° proof but they may be issued at 75, 80, 100 or even 106° proof (see Proof).

The Malt Whiskies

Malt whiskies are graded into three or four classes for blending purposes but different blenders may vary their gradings according to their availability to a particular blender. Some of the best whiskies are known as crackerjacks. In 1930 Mr Aeneas Macdonald gave the names of what he considered the thirteen best whiskies, but this must be considered quite unfair for there are several unmentioned whiskies such as Mortlach, Strathisla and Glen Mhor, which to-day are certainly quite as good. It may be that the better-known whiskies have rested a bit on their laurels and that some lesser-known ones have caught up.

The malt whiskies, since they are more expensive than blends, have a limited appeal and are not generally sold. They are available from Gordon & McPhail, and Campbell, Hope & King in Elgin, Strachan of Aboyne, Peter Thomson of Perth, and in Edinburgh from Muirheads, Dymock Howden, Lamberts and Hays, while in London they are to be found at Harrods, Fortnum & Mason, Robert Jackson, Peter Dominic and The Milroy's Soho Wine Market.

THE GLENLIVETS AND THEIR LIKE

The Glenlivet

No excuse is needed for giving these whiskies pride of place amongst the malts, for not only has Smith's Glenlivet been the queen of whiskies for over a hundred years but it has given its name to a whole family of whiskies. In 1880 under threat of legal proceedings an agreement was reached by which it became the only whisky entitled to call itself '*The Glenlivet*' as it was the only whisky made in the parish of Glenlivet, but other whiskies can use the name provided it is prefixed by another name. No fewer than 23 have availed themselves of the honour, and Glenlivet was called sarcastically the longest glen in Scotland. Some so-called Glenlivet distilleries are 20 miles distant and at least one Glenlivet distillery company hasn't even a distillery.

The Livet is a small tributary of the River Avon which enters the Spey half-way between Grantown-on-Spey and Craigellachie and collects water from the northern foothills of the Grampians. Before the days of the local railway and the motor car, this was indeed a remote area—a high barley-bearing plateau and not too far from the rich northern plain with good water and peat. It was ideally suited for illicit whisky making. Without a large-scale map it is difficult to find even now. In 1820 there were said to be 200 illicit stills in the area. The old Glenlivet distillery was at Drumin, a farm further up the hill than the present one. It was burnt down in 1858. The new one is in a commanding position like the old castles in its view. It stands strangely alone on the hillside.

Smith's Glenlivet Distillery was the first to be licensed, when the Government in 1823, on the recommendation of the Duke of Richmond and Gordon made an offer to license small distilleries cheaply. Prior to that, by a law of 1814, stills of under 500 gallons were illegal but that statute was generally ignored. In licensing his distillery the owner George Smith took considerable personal risk for he was considered by his neighbours to be a 'black leg'. He was, however, a robust Scot of the best type who was always prepared to defend his rights and especially his property. He also had the support of the local landowners who were anxious to 'clean up' the glen. Indeed one, the Laird of Aberlour, presented George Smith with a pair of pistols with which to defend himself. About this time one distillery on Deeside was actually burnt down by the objectors to regulation.

It was several years before the trouble died down, but the Smith family has continued in ownership ever since. They have also been prominent as farmers and in the conduct of local affairs. The history of the family is well given in the Glenlivet centenary volume published in 1924 (reprinted 1964) and in Bruce Lockhart's book.

'The Glenlivet' whisky has a deep mellowness and ripe fullness of flavour together with a delicacy of aroma which is easy to recognise. It has a subtle peatiness without being aggressively peaty and a gentle sweetness without any loss of freshness. A small quantity is bottled at twelve years old by the company and is issued with a yellow label, but other issues of mature whisky are bottled by Gordon & McPhail of Elgin. It is available at 70°, 80° and 100° proof. I have made experiments comparing all three and with knowledgeable friends have concluded that the 80° is certainly the best when each was diluted to 35°. There are however many inferior bottlings of less mature whiskies about, some of which are scarcely recognisable as 'The Glenlivet.'

The distillery does not use Livet water but draws supplies from local wells where peat and granite are not conspicuous. Its peat used to be local at Faemussachmoss but now comes from the great peat mosses at Pitsligo in Aberdeenshire. The Glenlivet Distillery is now part of the Glenlivet-Glen Grant Distillery Company, a public company quoted on the London Stock Exchange.

The distilleries that have found it desirable to use the name Glenlivet are: Macallan, Glen Grant, Dufftown, Longmorn, Glenburgie, Glendullan, Mortlach, Glen Elgin, Glendronach,

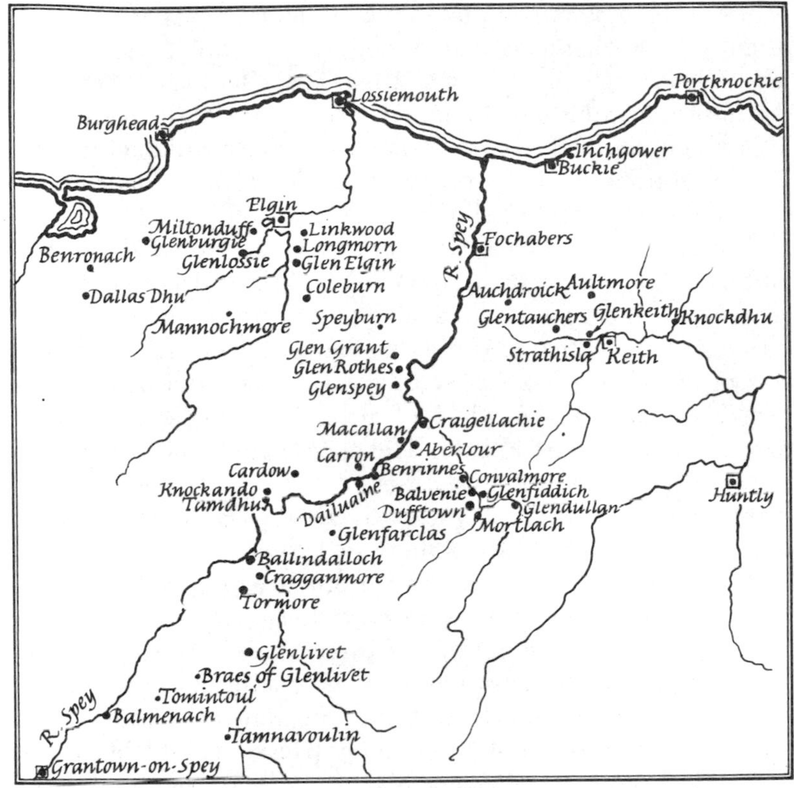

Detail of the Speyside distilleries

Glenfarclas, Glen Keith, Coleburn, Strathisla, Glen Rothes, Glen Moray, Aberlour, Tomintoul, Benromach, Milton Duff, Craigellachie, Aultmore, Dailuaine and Glenlossie. Even far-off Tomatin once described itself as in the Glenlivet area, but like Macallan it now considers itself of sufficient success not to use the name on the more modern labels. The D.C.L. distilleries have also given up the name Glenlivet. Only seven Glenlivets have survived to appear nowadays as single malts. Most are used for blending only and find a ready sale.

The Glenlivets, sometimes called the Glen Whiskies, in general have for a century maintained their quality and superiority.

They have a common fundamental flavour yet they differ slightly between themselves. I find, for example, Glen Grant and Glenfiddich slightly drier than The Glenlivet, Macallan, Dufftown, Strathisla or Longmorn. Some are more peaty than others. Those which are paler tend to be drier, although I have known bottlings which are very sweet. Very much depends on the kind of cask the whisky has been matured in.

It is hoped that the second century will see no further falling off in quality. According to the late Sir Robert Bruce Lockhart, a native of these parts and senior to me, Scotch whisky is not so good as it used to be. It may be that this is in part due to the use of the starch-rich barley of the Lothians and of England which produces a high yield of alcohol and a lighter whisky which matures more quickly. The poorer Highland barley has, on the other hand, relatively more fat and protein which contributes to the fruity flavour but at the same time makes heavier whisky which needs more maturing.

It is an unfortunate fact that so much whisky is being produced by the distilleries that they are short of storage space and sell it at the legal minimum of three years when it may be bottled with the distillery name. Some distilleries do their best by issuing distillery labels on condition that they are not used except for mature whisky. No malt whisky should be drunk before it is ten years old and this should be on the bottle. But alas this is not adhered to by buyers who may bottle or sell it at any time over the legal three years, so that a malt with a good name may sometimes seem very inferior.

Glen Grant-Glenlivet

Glen Grant may not be a place on the map but the fame of this whisky is sufficient to make people look for it, and the Grants of Strathspey have been making whisky legally or otherwise since the distilling began. It must be remembered, too, that in these parts a very large proportion of the population bears the noble name of Grant. Castle Grant is near Grantown-on-Spey.

Glen Grant-Glenlivet

The Glen Grant Distillery was founded by John and James Grant in 1840, but the brothers, who came from Inveravon further into the hills, appear to have been distilling on the farm of Dandaleith nearby from 1834. Since its foundation there has been a process of gradual modernisation. An unusual feature of the distillery is drum malting (see page 101). The credit for the fame of Glen Grant is given to a Mr George Grant who had been manager of Linkwood distillery nearby and became managing brewer at the age of twenty-four. He had made a special study of the art of distilling and made many changes in Glen Grant-Glenlivet Distillery.

The firm of J. & J. Grant, Glen Grant Ltd was formed in 1932 and in 1953 amalgamated with George and J. G. Smith of The Glenlivet to form The Glenlivet and Glen Grant Distilleries Ltd. In 1970 Longmorn and Hill Thomson (see page 19) became subsidiaries. The Distillers Company has a 14·5 per cent interest and Imperial Tobacco 11·5 per cent.

There was another distillery across the street in Rothes which had been begun by James Grant, son of the original founder, in 1897, but it was caught in the slump at the end of the century and closed down in 1901. In 1965 this was reopened after very complete modernisation with a large amount of automation. It has been given the name Caperdonich after the well from which both distilleries draw water.

Glen Grant whisky at its best has a distinction and flavour which is different from the other Glenlivets. Before the war many would have said it was the best malt and I still have some without a date of smooth almost unbelievable quality. There are on the market some fifteen to twenty Glen Grant whiskies from five to twenty-five years old with the distillery label, but alas 'there is nothing to prevent any owner of Glen Grant bottling at any other age over the legal minimum of three years',* although the distillery label is not issued under five years old. Some have been matured in sherry casks and some have not. The latter is pale and is rather a curiosity although it is not so good as the darker ones. The fifteen-year-old with

* Some other countries have a four- or five-year minimum.

the distillery label is the best but the older ones are scarcely worth the extra price. Considering how good it can be when it matures I think it is a pity to put it on the market at five and seven years although I am assured that the earlier ones are popular locally. They are of course cheaper!

The company has shown great wisdom in putting the age of the contents on the distillery labels but alas it is not on others. This is a practice that other distillers should copy. Glen Grant Malt Whisky is not to be confused with Grant's Glenfiddich or 'Grant's Standfast'—a blend.

Macallan

Here we have a whisky of quality in the best Speyside sense; indeed, many consider it now the best. It has a smooth richness of flavour quite its own. The distillery, like so many, had its origin on a farm. Macallan's farm is in the ancient Macallan parish on the hill just above the ford at Craigellachie near where the Telford bridge, built in 1814, now stands. The small old parish churchyard is within the distillery property. Here, in the late eighteenth century, cattle from the Morayshire coastal plain were assembled before crossing the river to the long drove road through the mountain passes to Falkirk and the other southern markets. It is easy to understand how the herdsmen spread the fame of this delicious whisky.

The distillery was one of the first (1824) to accept the Government offer to license distilleries for a small fee. In due course it passed into the hands of Alexander Reid, who had it till 1886 when it was sold to James Stuart. The latter sold it in 1892 to Roderick Kemp, who added to the buildings considerably. Kemp died in 1909 and the distillery was run by a trust for the family until 1946, when the private limited company of R. Kemp, Macallan Glenlivet Ltd was formed.* The present owners are descendants of Roderick Kemp. In 1965 the size of the distillery was doubled to meet the increasing demand.

Macallan has always maintained a high quality and has ensured that no whisky is issued as a single whisky at less than ten

* The company has now gone public with a capital of 2½ million pounds.

years old, but some is available at fifteen years and some even at over twenty-five. It is bottled at 70°, 80° and 100° proof and it is interesting to remark that after 120 years the firm has decided it can afford to drop the name Glenlivet from its label. I knew of no better malt whisky than Macallan's 1952 or 1953, but alas there is no more. Curiously enough the earlier ones have not the same delightful flavour nor has 1954. No explanation can be given for this.

Cardhu

This single malt had a rebirth in 1965, although a whisky Cardow but pronounced Carhu from the distillery was available earlier. When I first tasted it, I was not impressed. It seemed just another malt. Perhaps the expensive new advertisements had made me expect too much! Later, however, when I took it after a blend and with haggis it was much more worthy. This emphasises the point that a whisky may taste quite differently according to its accompaniments and the circumstances in which it is taken. Cardhu is a good Speyside whisky but does not claim to be a Glenlivet.

Distilling appears to have been going on in this remote area from quite early times but the first legal distillery at Cardow was founded there by John Cumming in 1824. Its whisky soon acquired a good reputation and was taken by horse and cart to the little port of Burghead on the north coast of Morayshire and thence shipped to Leith.

The distillery has a striking situation at Knockando overlooking the Spey valley at Craigellachie, and its beautifully kept still-house, with five great shining copper stills in a row, is a really magnificent sight.

It was bought from the Cumming family in 1893 by John Walker of Kilmarnock and its whisky no doubt became part of the famous Johnnie Walker blends.

Tamdhu

This is a delightful little farm-like distillery down the hill in the woods below its great neighbour Cardhu.

It has been owned by Highland Distilleries almost since its inception by the Tamdhu Distillery Company in 1897, who worked it only for one year. This small company with a capital of only £19,200 was subscribed to by well-known distillers such as Dewar of Perth, Sanderson of Leith, Robertson of Glasgow and Walker of Kilmarnock, and had as its chairman William Grant, banker of Elgin. No shareholder held more than £2,000 and they rapidly sold out.

The whisky is typically Speyside with a good flavour and not too peaty. Malt is made by the Saladin method. So far as I can find it is bottled as a single only by William Cadenhead of Aberdeen.

Glenfarclas Glenlivet

This is a typical Speyside distillery. It was begun in 1836 by a Robert Hay, who died in 1865, when it was bought by John Grant, farmer at Blairfindy, who established the present firm of J. & G. Grant whose charming descendants still run it. An earlier William Grant carried arms in Prince Charlie's army in 1745 and afterwards 'submitted to the King's mercy'. The distillery stands up off the main road on a somewhat isolated, exposed and windy site on the hillside at Ballindalloch, near where the River Avon joins the Spey. Water and peat were at first obtained locally—indeed the distillery is almost surrounded by moors, but now the malt comes from Kircaldy. The distillery probably developed from a farm on the rich lands streaming from the great hills beyond, the home of the golden eagle, the wild cat, the ptarmigan and the red deer. It is now a most progressive distillery and it is slowly being reconstructed and modernised.

The whisky is a fine full-flavoured malt, so popular with blenders, indeed, that most is sold before it is made, but some is available by bottle under the distillery label bottled by Gordon & McPhail at 70°, 100° and at an unusual 105° proof. I find that Glenfarclas 1955 at 80° bottled by the Grant Bonding Co., is the best whisky since Macallan 1952.

Tormore

This whisky, which has recently come on the retail market, is made in the very elegant new distillery built in 1958 by Seager Evans (see page 89), the maker of Long John. It is a robust Speyside whisky called after the nearby great hill and made with water from the Loch of Gold. Without having a noticeable peaty or other distinctive flavour it is a whisky with an appeal. It has a really rich flavour and is issued at 75° proof. The distillery is described in relation to Seager Evans.

Longmorn-Glenlivet

Longmorn on the main road about half-way between Rothes and Elgin has long been recognised by the connoisseur to produce one of the best Glenlivets. It is owned by Longmorn-Glenlivet Distillery Company which also has Ben Riach Distillery. It was built in 1893–4 but on the site there has been a water-driven meal mill since about 1600. This still stands and is used as a dwelling house.

The name is probably Welsh from 'Lhanmorgund'—Morgund, or Morgan, the holy man. A warehouse now stands on what is a reputed chapel area. The water comes from a local spring which never dries and the peat is obtained from the nearby Mannoch Hill.

The whisky, sold at 70° proof, has perhaps not the rich flavour of Smith's Glenlivet or Macallan's but it has an outstanding bouquet worthy of a brandy glass after dinner. A mixture of these whiskies with Longmorn with perhaps a dash of Clynelish makes what is probably the best possible drink in the world. In 1970 Longmorn together with Hill Thomson, which for many years had an interest in it, became subsidiaries of the Glen Grant-Glenlivet combine.

Linkwood

This charming little distillery is in a wood near Elgin and has recently been reconditioned by Scottish Malt Distillers. The distillery was built in 1821 and is named after an old mansion house on the site, but little appears to be known about its beginnings. The reputation of Linkwood whisky was made by Mr Roderick Mackenzie, a Gaelic-speaking native of Wester Ross who for many years supervised its making 'with unremitting vigilance'. Not one item of equipment was ever replaced unless it had to be and it is said not even a spider's web could be removed. Linkwood is a pleasant light whisky with a typical Glenlivet flavour although it reminds me of the Lowland Rosebank. It is not a well-known whisky but has long been classified as one of the best, but it varies very much. I have known Linkwood produce a really superb whisky but, as the year was not on the bottle, I cannot identify it.

Tomatin

It is a surprise to find a distillery at Tomatin (pronounced like the fruit) 1,500 feet high on the northern slopes of the Grampian Mountains about 19 miles south of Inverness. It was based on a fifteenth-century distillery which supplied the needs of men attending the small local market before they and their animals began their long trek south through the hills. It was remodelled about 1909 and of more recent years has been in the forefront of modernisation which has made it the largest malt distillery. It can yield over 1,000,000 proof gallons of whisky each year. This has been made possible by mechanisation at all stages. The still-house has five wash and four spirit stills, a most impressive sight. All are heated by oil burners mechanically controlled from a centre.

Tomatin is owned by a public company, quoted on the London Stock Exchange. It has a capital of over two and a half million pounds.

Like the distillery, the whisky has an individuality born of local peat and local water which passes, as the whisky pundits say it should, through peat over red granite. Unfortunately in a dry year water becomes scarce. This is a fact which emphasises the necessity for a distillery to be near an abundant water supply, but I find it strange that no distillery I know of cools the still effluent electrically. Perhaps it would be too expensive.

Tomatin describes itself as a light bodied and peaty flavoured malt which makes it very popular with blenders. It is a good example of a dry single malt well matured, although its flavour, which is not unlike a Glenlivet, is somewhat obscured by the peat.

The Blair Athol

The Blair Athol Distillery is surprisingly not in the village of that name but some 11 miles south at the lower end of beautiful Pitlochry. It produces one of the best single malts and is now issued at 70° proof. A bottle of the old 80° is more worth drinking for its fullness and flavour gave a distinction not commonly found. The new 70° has not the same character. This appears to be true of many malts (see Glenlivet). The whisky is now more like that of Dufftown than it used to be.

Strictly speaking this whisky is not a Glenlivet but is of the same type.

The distillery itself, although small, is almost a model distillery. Nestling into the side of a wooded hill it is beautifully kept and sets out to make visitors welcome. It is of interest that the water supply of the town of Pitlochry is good enough to be extensively used for diluting the fresh whisky, but in addition the distillery has a much earlier supply from a local burn which passes through the distillery from the lower reaches of Ben Vrackie on its way to the nearby River Tummel.

The distillery is owned by Arthur Bell & Sons of Perth, who also have Dufftown Glenlivet Distillery (see page 25) and Inchgower Distillery at Buckie. With three such distilleries it is no wonder that Bell's blended whiskies are popular.

Glen Mhor

From the banks of the Caledonian Canal at Inverness comes Glen Mhor, named after the Great Glen which runs west to Fort William. It is made with water from Loch Ness of monster fame. Here we have a whisky of real merit made by the Birnie family since 1892. The late amiable William Birnie made a study of the statistics of whisky and has been the great pessimist, suggesting that since stocks are accumulating whisky is being over-produced and that there will be a glut as there was in 1900. There certainly will never be a glut of delicious Glen Mhor. While it cannot be said to have any outstanding flavour it has an honest subtle richness and 'fatness' reminiscent of the patina of old furniture, which it owes to the care with which it is made and the fact that it is so well matured before it is sold. This is a feature which the demand for whisky makes rare. To appreciate Glen Mhor at its best I advise taking it after one of the standard blends. Then one appreciates the words of Neil Gunn, the Scottish novelist, just after speaking of Glen Mhor, 'that until a man has the luck to chance on a perfectly matured malt, he does not really know what whisky is'.

Like Blair Athol it is not really a Glenlivet but can be conveniently put in the same class. It can be described as a little more robust. A little added to John Haig makes a lovely smooth drink, the cheapest de luxe.

It was at Glen Mhor that the method of malting in Saladin boxes was first used.

The distillery was built by Birnie & Mackinlay, but now is owned by John Walker (D.C.L.). The whisky, which is available in Scottish shops, is bottled at 75° proof.

FETTERCAIRN

This Kincardine distillery is at the eastern end of the Grampians. The original building was established in 1820 by the brothers Guthrie who were born at nearby Brechin. Their brother was the famous divine Dr Thomas Guthrie, a great orator and promoter of temperance and social reforms. He is remembered in Edinburgh by his statue in Princes Street Gardens and by Guthrie's Boys Band. In 1824 the distillery was moved to a region nearer Laurencekirk on the picturesque River Esk which supplies its water. The distillery was the first to use oil heating of the stills. The malt is now bought.

This whisky is, I think, the best of the eastern malts now available, with a full, dry flavour, but it is in short supply. It is issued at 75° proof at eight years old, and hence the label 'Fettercairn 875'. The distillery is now owned, together with Dalmore and Tomintoul, was bought by 'Suits' (Scotland and Universal Investment Trust) in 1971.

It is of interest that when the Fettercairn company was first formed in 1887, it had as its chairman Sir John R. Gladstone, who owned the nearby Fasque estates which had been bought in 1829 by John Gladstone, the father of William Ewart Gladstone, the great Liberal Prime Minister, responsible for the greatly beneficial Spirits Act of 1860. This not only abolished taxes on malt, but made possible the selling of whisky by the bottle and the making of spirituous liquors. He was indeed a good friend of whisky.

GLENGOYNE

This whisky is made in a little gem of a distillery in a valley in the Campsie Hills in the south of Stirlingshire where whisky has been made since 1873. Until about 1895 it was known as Glen Guin.

In 1876 it was bought by the enterprising Lang Brothers,

wine merchants in the Broomielaw of Glasgow, who began blending in the basement of the Argyle Free Kirk. Indeed, they eventually took over the whole church, thereby subtly blending 'spirit of wine with spirit divine'. It remained very much a family business until 1965, when the company became one of the Robertson & Baxter group (see page 84), but the third generation of the Lang family are still intimately concerned. The distillery is a showpiece, many of its rooms are tiled and it is all beautifully kept. It is nothing like a Speyside distillery! Up the valley is its dam filled by water from the hills above, and there is a charming chalet for the entertainment of guests. Its malt is made elsewhere.

It is proud of the fact that the father of the late Lord Tedder, Marshal of the R.A.F. during the second world war, was an excise officer here. Lord Tedder subsequently became a director of D.C.L.

At 80° proof, the whisky is a very pleasant sweetish and gentle malt with no outstanding flavour. Although the whisky is technically just a Highland malt, it is fair to say that in many instances it is bought and used as a Lowland malt for blending.

Glen Rothes

This is a typical delicious Speyside whisky, but mostly goes for blending, but it can be found. The distillery, recently reconditioned, is owned by Highland Distilleries of Glasgow.

THE DUFFTOWN AND NEARBY MALTS

If we leave the Spey at Craigellachie and go east by the Dufftown road we cannot miss the newly modernised D.C.L. Distillery just above the village. Its great gleaming copper stills of gigantic proportions stare through an enormous window. In due course at the top of a hill we look into the unique whisky basin of Dufftown with its six distilleries, Convalmore, Balvenie, Glenfiddich, Dufftown, Mortlach and Glendullan. In the little town of three wide streets there is scarcely a person to be seen and, still more remarkable, it is impossible to buy all its local products by the bottle. It is full of whisky stories. I like that one of war-time when petrol was scarce and whisky went by train. It was said that the inhabitants always knew about the departure of a whisky train by the noise of the unusual amount of shunting, and were always ready with all kinds of receptacles in case a wagon leaked!

It is easy to understand how this area became a centre of distilleries. It has abundant water, peat and once enough local barley. It is one of the most remote parts of Scotland. To east and south roads pass out into the northern slopes of the lesser Grampians where there is scarcely a house or a motor car to be seen on the beautiful and good roads between the hills. A little further on we come to Tomintoul, the highest village in Scotland. There can be no more pleasant drive than this in early September when the hills are purple with heather.

THE DUFFTOWN-GLENLIVET

Dufftown, situated in the very heart of the malt whisky distilling industry, has two beautiful glens in the vicinity, Glenfiddich and Dullan; it is in the latter glen through which flows the Dullan water that the Dufftown-Glenlivet Distillery is located. The water used for mashing comes from 'Jock's

Well', famous in the district for producing a plenteous supply that is ideally suitable for distilling purposes.

The distillery was founded in 1887 by a syndicate which a few years later was formed into a company as P. Mackenzie & Co., Distillers Limited. Arthur Bell & Sons Ltd acquired the distillery in 1933. This firm is described later.

Since Bell became proprietors, the distillery has had a number of improvements made to it, also additional warehouses have been completed. 'Dufftown-Glenlivet' is a typical peaty Speyside malt that is much sought after by blenders, but it is marketed as a single malt at 80° proof.

Glenfiddich and Balvenie

The story of William Grant of Glenfiddich is indeed fascinating. He was born in 1839, the son of a poor soldier who served with Wellington in the Peninsular War, and after leaving the local school in Dufftown he was apprenticed to a shoemaker but later became the manager of a lime works. He had hoped to set up a lime works for himself, but having no capital he eventually in 1866 entered Mortlach distillery where he worked for twenty years, during which time, being of studious habit, he not only learnt all he could about distilling and construction, but with Scottish thrift saved some money.

His chance came when he was able to buy the equipment of the old Cardow Distillery for £120 and with his sons and a little outside help he built Glenfiddich Distillery, which began work in 1887. In the financing of the distillery he was assisted by his two eldest sons, one of whom had become a lawyer and the other a schoolmaster. With three of his younger sons he ran the distillery for the first two years, during which two of these three sons prepared themselves for entrance to Aberdeen University where they eventually became doctors of medicine. The third son after a period at sea bought nearby Glendronach Distillery.

Glenfiddich Distillery having such a founder flourished from the beginning, so much so that in 1894 another distillery,

Balvenie, was built a little down the hill. Both are on the little River Fiddich which flows into the Spey. In spite of his great work William Grant lived till 1923 when he was eighty-three.

In 1955 the Glenfiddich Distillery was rebuilt to double its capacity and with Balvenie, which also had been added to, it has twelve stills and is now one of the largest Highland malt distilleries. The original small but very solid office of William Grant, however, still stands. Recently an old barn has been attractively adorned as a reception centre for parties with attendants in Highland dress who make you very welcome.

In 1962 the company took another leap forward by building on a very large site of 64 acres a great new grain whisky distillery at Girvan in Ayrshire incorporating the Lowland malt distillery of Ladyburn. Now a rectifying unit for the making of gin has been added. The grain distillery was built in nine months instead of the normal two years and cost £1,250,000.

The whisky produced to-day is Glenfiddich Straight Malt at 10–11 years old, in a triangular bottle at 70° proof. I describe it as a good fruity Glenlivet-like whisky with a distinctly peaty flavour, but it does not use the name Glenlivet. Balvenie whisky has a quite different flavour and no one knows why, a fact so common amongst the products of nearby distilleries and indeed of nearby vineyards. Why it is bottled only at 106·4° proof I am not quite sure. This is the concentration at which it comes from the still, 'As we get it' the bottler Macfarlane Bruce & Co. say, but it is not sufficiently aromatic to be used as brandy.

With such good sources of malts and grain whisky Grants is well placed for the production of its blended whisky 'Standfast'. The name is from the battle cry of the Clan Grant 'Standfast Craigellachie', but I must confess I prefer the delicious Straight Malt which is a good traditional Speyside whisky.

Mortlach

The four whiskies from the Dufftown basin show again how malt whiskies made apparently by the same process can be so similar yet so different. They are all excellent whiskies of the Glenlivet type. Glenfiddich I find the driest, Dufftown the more peaty and Mortlach the most fruity and lush with more peat than it used to have.

Mortlach Distillery has an interesting history. It was in this dell that Malcolm the Second, the Scottish king, defeated the Danes in the year 1010 by damming up the little River Dullan a mile up-stream. The Danes, attracted by the pleasant bowl, camped in it—the word Mortlach means the bowl-shaped valley —but at night the dam was broken and the Danes were overwhelmed by the water and the Scots. As a thanksgiving for the victory Malcolm added '3 spears' length' to Mortlach Church, which had been founded in 566. The distillery has recently been reconditioned by Scottish Malt Distillers, not to increase its output as has been the case with so many reconstructions, but simply because its walls were crumbling. It will be interesting to compare to-day's excellent whisky with that fifteen years hence—so keep a bottle. The Distillers Company is about to build a new malt distillery at nearby Glendullan where it already has a small distillery.

Strathisla-Glenlivet

This is a rich full-flavoured whisky in the best tradition of the Glenlivets although made at Keith, a considerable distance from the Livet. Anyone drinking the fifteen years old for the first time will remark on its excellence, which is somewhat that of Mortlach.

Strathisla is one of the oldest distilleries in Scotland and looks it. It was established in 1786 by William Longmore, whose name is well remembered in Keith as a public benefactor. Keith is in the centre of the great barley-growing plain in the north of Banffshire and is of considerable historical interest, having associations with the great Montrose in the reign of Charles the Second.

The distillery was originally called Milton and its appearance is in the best Glenlivet tradition with an air of careless antiquity a state encouraged by the remarkable Mr Bronfman of Seagrams of Canada.

In 1950 the distillery was acquired by Chivas Brothers of Aberdeen, which has now become part of Seagrams. Its name was changed to Strathisla and a little later (1957) a new distillery called Glen Keith was built across the little River Isla on the site of an old meal and flour mill. Here malting is done by the Saladin method and the dried malt piped across the river to Strathisla. In due course the whiskies in cask go to Paisley and Aberdeen, where bottling is done (see page 91).

Chivas Brothers who market the blend 'Chivas Regal' began as wine merchants and grocers in Aberdeen in 1841, when James Chivas with Charles Stewart took over the business of William Edward which had been established in 1801. This no doubt accounts for the date on the bottle. Since blends were unknown at that time what whisky was sold is uncertain, but the firm claim that the name Regal has long been used. It must have been very different from the Chivas Regal blend of to-day, in the development of which Mr Bronfman himself played a leading part about 1950. Chivas Regal is a rich blend based no doubt on Strathisla, to which not only grain whisky but a number of really mature malts have been added. It has a delicious flavour but it is unduly expensive. The Royal Warrant was granted to James Chivas as a purveyor to Queen Victoria in 1843. The partnership was dissolved in 1857 and James took his brother John into the business and it remained in the family till Alexander, the son of the founder, died in 1893.

The business continued as Chivas Brothers under new management in which a William Mitchel played a leading part and eventually became sole director in 1935. A further Royal Warrant was granted in 1925. In 1936 the firm was sold to a limited company and in 1950 it passed into the control of Seagrams of Canada, when the new era of expansion began.

Aultmore

Here is another excellent malt but it is not yet available in London.

Aultmore Distillery near Keith was built by Alexander Edward of Sanquhar, Forres, during the years 1895–6, and in July 1897 distilling was started. Up to 1899 Mr Edward was the sole proprietor but, on his acquisition of Oban Distillery in that year, he floated a limited liability company called The Oban and Aultmore Glenlivet Distillery Company Limited of which he was managing director.

In 1923 Aultmore Distillery was sold to John Dewar & Sons Limited, from whom it was purchased by Scottish Malt Distillers Limited in October 1930 and licensed to John & Robt. Harvey & Company Limited.

In 1972 the distillery received a face-lift like its neighbour Glentauchers.

Oban

This distillery has recently been reopened and issues its whisky locally in a decanter shaped bottle by John Hopkins of Glasgow.

Glendullan

This is described in the supplement.

THE NORTHERN MALTS

These excellent malt whiskies are not so well known as those from the Spey and have less uniformity. Most go into the blends.

OLD PULTENEY

This whisky comes from farthest north, from Wick, the county town of Caithness, and is only available locally. It is a whisky of considerable distinction having a succession of flavours and not noticeably peaty; indeed, one is tempted to think that a good whisky could be made without peat at all.

It is to me quite surprising that such a good whisky could be made in this grim, windswept fishing town on the North Sea. Caithness is indeed a bare county and needs a good whisky to warm it up. Dr. Neil Gunn, a native of these parts, recognised in Old Pulteney when well matured 'some of the strong characteristics of the northern temperament. It has to be come upon as one comes upon a friend and treated with proper respect.' It is a pity that there is not more of it in the south, but it must be remembered that the Scots do not export all their best products.

Like so many distilleries Pulteney was closed down for many years (1926–51) and a part of it became a meal mill. A few years ago it was reopened and is now owned by Hiram Walker (see page 94). Old Pulteney no doubt contributes to the blend 'Old Smuggler' and Ballantines.

CLYNELISH

This is quite distinctly tasty whisky from the little coal-mining town of Brora on the coast of Sutherland. It was a favourite whisky of the great Victorian connoisseur Professor Saintsbury. It is of interest that the distillery was built in 1819 by the Duke of Sutherland, when Marquis of Stafford, to provide a use for the barley grown by the tenants of his farms. His great Dunrobin Castle, once the home of the family, is nearby but it is now a school. The Distillers Company have recently built nearby a new distillery called Brora to provide a similar whisky which is so valuable for blending. Clynelish whisky is certainly the most fully flavoured whisky outside Islay and one is tempted to think that the peat mosses from which the peat is obtained used to grow seaweed. It is a little reminiscent of Laphroaig but less peaty. It is a man's whisky but not to everyone's taste. I find it fruity and delicious. It is now owned by The Distillers Company and it is bottled by Ainslie at 70° proof. Better bottling at 80° is available at the Royal Marine Hotel, and the Sutherland Arms, in Brora.

Professor Saintsbury in 1920 recommended a mixture of Clynelish and Smith's Glenlivet.

It is a pleasant run up the eastern shore of the Cromarty Firth to Alness and after passing the flat land it is not surprising to find two distilleries at Alness, Dalmore and Teaninich. The whisky from the latter is not on the retail market and goes for blending. The distillery belongs to the D.C.L. group.

The three Cromarty whiskies which are available are quite distinct from each other and are again good examples of how different whiskies from the same area can be.

Dalmore

This might be described as a good solid dry whisky with slightly peaty flavour, a man's whisky, a little reminiscent of Cardhu. The later vintages are however less peaty. It is said to mature in the minimum three years but it is issued at from eight to twenty years old.

All three distilleries were built about the same time. Dalmore, now the largest, was founded in 1839 on the site of a famous old meal mill but was taken over by the Mackenzie family in 1867. They have maintained an active interest in it ever since and under the direction of the present chairman, who took over from his father in 1946, the distillery has been greatly modernised. The handling of the barley has been quite changed, while the Saladin method of malting and mechanical stoking have been introduced. Dalmore is fortunate in having a wonderful site on the shores of the Cromarty Firth looking across to the Black Isle. At an early date it was fortunate to acquire the sole water rights of the River Alness and it can discharge its effluent into the sea. Two of the 1874 stills are still in use and with two larger ones the output of the plant has grown enormously. In 1971 the distillery was bought by 'Suits' (Scottish and Universal Investments Trusts).

GLENMORANGIE

This whisky is much more delicate and mild, almost like a Lowland malt. It ought to mature early but it also is issued at ten years old.

The Glenmorangie Distillery Company was formed in 1887 to take over the interests of the Mathieson family. The area has an excellent water and peat supply but it is now found easier to bring the peat from Pitsligo in Aberdeenshire like so many other distilleries. Like its neighbour Balblair it is a very self-contained little distillery and it was one of the first distilleries to use steam-heated stills which are now so popular. In 1918 the distillery was bought by Macdonald & Muir of Leith, who also own Glen Moray Glenlivet distillery and are blenders.

BALBLAIR

This is a more flavoured whisky, almost without any peat but very slightly aromatic. This may be because the distillery uses a local very soft friable peat which may contain a plant responsible for its pleasant unusualness.

Glenmorangie is just across the peninsula. Distilling began here as a side-line to farming at Morangie, which is about a mile and a half north of Tain. The distillery also has a lovely site looking across the Dornoch Firth to the hills of Sutherland. It was originally a brewery but was converted in 1842 by a Mr William Mathieson and his brother.

I have been unable to obtain much history of Balblair which is reputed to have been established in 1790. It is in the country a few miles west of Glenmorangie with a similar pleasant outlook. In 1840 the distillery was controlled by Andrew Ross & Son but subsequently passed into the hands of the Cumming family, who at one time also had Old Pulteney in Wick; now bought in 1970 by Hiram Walker (see page 94).

THE LOWLAND MALTS

It is of some interest that the Lowland malts were the first whiskies to be drunk in quantity in England, and about 1850 most larger towns in the south of Scotland had a distillery. The Lowland malts are more gentle than the Highland malts and are said to mature quicker. Yet to-day there is not even one in Dumfries where Robert Burns was an exciseman and wrote many of his poems. Near Kirkcudbright there is an area called 'The Stell' where a still used to be.

In 1906 there were two distilleries in Langholm, one in Annan and seven in Lanarkshire. All have disappeared. Only four Lowland malts are now available as singles, Rosebank, Bladnoch, Auchentoshan and Littlemill, the last two only recently. The whiskies from the others, which are in the neighbourhood of Edinburgh and Glasgow, all go for blending. They give a slight brandy-like flavour to blends.

Bladnoch

In its heyday this was a very good whisky with a wonderful bouquet, but the old mature variety is no longer available except very privately. Fortunately I have a little over thirty years old which now smells like the best cognac although it is tasteless. The distillery has only been reopened a few years ago after being reconditioned. The whisky on the market has not been matured long enough to allow an opinion to be given of its real quality. It would probably be worth while laying it down.

Bladnoch Distillery is at the lower end of the village of that name and has a pleasant site on the Bladnoch river from whence it draws its water. It is about one mile from the town of Wigtown, which is the county town of one of the least spoiled counties in Britain. The distillery was opened by the local McClelland family in 1818 and for many years it flourished, but like so many small distilleries it fell on evil days in the

1930's and closed down. In 1956 the somewhat derelict premises were bought by A. B. Grant, a large blending and exporting firm of Glasgow, who put new plant into it with, I believe, the first oil heating. It was sold again in 1964 to McGowan & Cameron, blenders and wholesalers of Glasgow, who have doubled its output by utilising the old malting house and buying malt. It still retains its striking red doors which were mentioned by Barnard, who in 1887 described most of the distilleries of Scotland. The distillery was bought by Inver House in 1972.

Rosebank

This is an excellent light flavoured whisky, somewhat reminiscent of Glenmorangie. It used to be described as a 'silent malt'. It is easy to understand why such a light whisky was preferred in England to the old and sterner Highland malts before modern blends became available, although modern Highland malts, when matured, are very different to the ones that were then available.

Rosebank is on the banks of the old Forth and Clyde canal, about one mile north of Falkirk.

As early as 1798 distilling was carried out in this area by the Stark Brothers, but in 1840 the distillery became the property of the Rankin family, who reconditioned it in 1864. This has again been done by D.C.L. The distillery however scarcely lives up to its beautiful name. It is a dismal cramped place and roses are not conspicuous.

A visit to Rosebank makes an interesting trip, especially if we cross from the south by the new Forth Bridge and recross the river 15 miles further up by the Kincardine Bridge, visiting on the way the very beautiful reconditioned Stuart period village of Culross.

Glenkinchie deserves special mention as it is the showpiece of the Distillers Company, nestling in a tiny glen near Pencaitland in East Lothian with two gardeners to maintain appearances, and a bowling green for the Staff. It makes an easy trip from Edinburgh. The distillery was built by a local farmer about

1840 and is situated in one of the richest agricultural areas in Scotland. The whisky produced is said to be a distinguished Lowland malt, but alas it all goes to the blenders. It is licensed to John Haig.

Ladyburn at Girvan, which is adjacent to Grant's great grain distillery there, stands on what is probably the grandest and largest distillery site, looking across the coast to Ailsa Craig and Arran. Its products will go into the excellent blends of W. Grant.

Perhaps one day the Lowland malts will again come into their own. They are still being made and used in enormous quantities, but they never get time to mature and, like the grain whiskies, are never mentioned in advertisements. Blenders seem to resent their mention, preferring to state that their products are 'based on Highland malts'!

The Dumbarton Malts

If we cross the Clyde between Glasgow and Greenock we reach the beautiful county of Dumbarton lying between lovely Loch Long and bonnie Loch Lomond, where from its Kirkpatrick hills we see the peaks of the lower Grampians. The county is partly Lowland and partly Highland; indeed, it is on the imaginary Highland Line which runs from Dundee to Greenock which divides the Highlands and the Lowlands, and below which it is 'not done' to wear the kilt unless you are Highland born. Glasgow and Fife are not thereby Highland.

The whiskies are likewise, quite different from the Highland malts yet not quite Lowland malts. Whisky has been made in this area since whisky was first made but many distilleries have disappeared. Most of the whisky made goes for blending (see Hiram Walker), but the appearance of some on the retail market signifies the increasing desire for single malts. Only two are available on the retail market, Littlemill and Auchentoshan.

Auchentoshan

This distillery is in what must have been a lovely glen overlooking the Clyde some 10 miles north of Glasgow, adjacent to the great new Erskine Bridge. It was one of the few distilleries bombed during the war, when the stream ran with blazing whisky! Although founded by Thorne in 1825 it has only had three owners, the longest being MacLachlans, who operated it for eighty-nine years. In 1969 it was purchased by Eadie Cairns, the owner of a large number of licensed houses in Glasgow, who has set about giving the distillery a new image inside and out. Much of its apparatus has been replaced. The distillery which is of moderate size is one of the few which has three stills, wash 4,100 gallons, low wines 2,300 gallons and spirit 2,300 gallons.

Its whisky, which has only recently become available as a single Lowland malt, has a delightful flavour and there is little wonder that it is so popular with blenders. Cairns Blend made by the company, to which other whiskies have been added, is scarcely worthy of its parent malt.

Littlemill

Littlemill is at Bowling near the town of Dumbarton on the northern bank of the Clyde in a most delightful situation, but alas the site is split by a very busy road.

It was built about 1750 by George Buchanan, a maltster from Glasgow, but was greatly enlarged in 1875 by a Mr Hay, later Hay Farmers & Co., and peat was imported from Orkney, but now malt is bought.

Originally the distillery made beer for the monks of Paisley Abbey 'across the water'. As early as 1821 Littlemill was making 20,000 proof gallons of whisky annually. After passing through several ownerships, including Mackinlay & Birnie of Inverness, it closed down in the depression of 1929, but in 1931 it was reopened by Cecil Fausett and Duncan G. Thomas, an American of Scottish origin. In 1958 Fausett sold his interest to what is now Barton Brands of Chicago and Kentucky, who since the death of Mr Thomas have acquired the remainder.

The present distillery owes its somewhat unusual design to Mr Thomas, who pioneered so many ideas in the making of whisky, especially a method of racking and a design of Saladin tank. The distillery makes three whiskies in the same plant by mixing the output of its three stills and varying its peating—Littlemill, Dunglass and Glenbank. Only Littlemill is on the market as a single malt. It has the lovely brandy flavour of a good Lowland malt but is put on the market too young, and alas its old whiskies have been rapidly taken up by the blenders. I feel that this is a sad position, for the reputation of any distillery depends on there being available fully matured samples of its products.

The distillery works in conjunction with Loch Lomond Distillery (not to be confused with Lomond Distillery) at Alexandria, where is a modern blending and bottling plant.

Two of the other Lowland distilleries are controlled by Scottish Malt Distillers (i.e. D.C.L.), St Magdelene at Linlithgow and Glenkinchie near Edinburgh. Hiram Walker owns two, Inverleven and Lomond near Dumbarton. Ladyburn at Girvan (Ayrshire) is controlled by W. Grant.

THE CAMPBELTOWN MALTS

The story of the disappearance of thirty-two distilleries at Campbeltown is not only a very sad story but may even be a warning for the present. At the beginning of the century the little Royal Burgh at the south end of the Kintyre Peninsula was indeed the whisky capital of Scotland. From the point of view of whisky making Campbeltown is ideal. It has good supplies of water, coal and peat and in early days much of its barley was grown locally. It is rather a surprise to see so much arable land in such a western place but no doubt the Gulf Stream makes it warmer than it otherwise would be. 'Success, however, contained the seeds of destruction' for some distilleries, in order to satisfy demand, began to put poor spirit into poor casks to satisfy the rapidly growing population of Glasgow and its whisky speculators.

There was a time when the Campbeltown malts were known as the Hector of the West, the deepest voice of the choir—a compliment indeed. When the financial slump came in the late 1920's the public and the blenders became more choosey and turned up their noses at the Campbeltown 'stinking fish', especially when plenty of good whisky from the Highlands was available. The poor distilleries destroyed the reputation of the others, a warning indeed to the many blenders to-day who are harming if not destroying the reputation of Scotch whisky, especially abroad. I have personally purchased undrinkable whisky abroad when I had every reason to believe it really was made in Scotland. We must only hope that the tragic story of Campbeltown does not repeat itself in a more general way.

Thirty years ago twelve distilleries remained but to-day there are only two, Springbank and Glen Scotia.

Springbank

This was the one Campbeltown malt good enough to be the only distillery to survive the debacle. It was built in 1823 by the Mitchell family. The Mitchells were orginally farmers, and their descendants still own and control it; a most unique record. The distillery has of recent years been very extensively modernised, yet in spite of great shortage of space the importance of the traditional floor malting is still insisted upon and its wash still is most unusual in being heated not only by coal but also by steam-heated coils. It has two spirit stills, one of which is used for the redistillation of foreshots and feints. This process probably contributes to its lightness. Springbank whisky is a full-flavoured, very pleasant, light whisky somewhat reminiscent of Rosebank, the Lowland malt. It also makes Glen Extra.

Glen Scotia

This whisky is very different from Springbank. It is heavier, strongly flavoured and somewhat reminiscent of an 'oily' Irish whiskey, and we have to remember that Campbeltown is only some 30 miles from Northern Ireland. Malt is no longer made but is bought from Hutchisons of Kirkcaldy, Fife.

So far as I can discover they both use similar peat and water, the only difference being the separate distillation of foreshots. Glen Scotia, which began as Scotia, is the only old distillery to be reopened.

The distillery, which has changed hands many times, was built in 1832 by Stewart Galbraith & Co. in the vicinity of the historic Parliament Square where, in the year 503, Fergus, the first King of Scotland, built his Parliament House and from which the affairs of Scotland were administered till 843. Tradition has it that the famous coronation stone of Scone came from here. At the end of the first world war the distillery was sold to West Highland Malt Distilleries, who in turn sold to Duncan MacCallum in 1924, but from 1928 to 1933 the distillery was closed. MacCallum died in 1930 and his trustees sold it to Bloch

Bros., who in 1954 sold it with Scapa Distillery in Orkney and stocks to Hiram Walker. The present owner is A. Gillies & Co., who bought it in 1955. The distillery was described by Barnard in 1887 as being 'situated at the end of a subway and seems to have hidden itself away as if the making of whisky at the time was bound to be kept a dark secret'.

Campbeltown looks a long way away on the map but the journey there by car from Tarbert at the top of Loch Fyne is very worthwhile. The tip of the peninsula with its pleasant climate and quaint little town and harbour with many fishing boats and yachts is of another world, more reminiscent of the south of England than of Scotland. Its own whiskies can be bought locally.

THE ISLAND MALTS

Most of these are produced on the remote island of Islay which is in the Atlantic to the west of the Mull of Kintyre, and which is remarkable for having eight distilleries. Several were, until recently, out of action, but with the greatly increased popularity of whisky some of these have been reconditioned and are in use again. How these have survived considering that twenty distilleries in nearby Campbeltown on the mainland have disappeared is difficult to explain.

The Islay malts have got something, but unfortunately only four are generally available. These whiskies may be described as powerful and for strong men. Some have more than an aggressive, peaty flavour. Most people say they taste medicinal, something like an antiseptic, so much so that they are harsh and to some people pungent and unpleasant.

The gem is the little distillery of Caol Ila which nestles on the Sound of Jura on the east side of the island. It has its private wharf by which it imports its barley and from which it exports its whisky. The distillery was taken over in 1887 by Bulloch, Lade & Co., a blending company which became part of The Distillers Company in 1927.

No island in the world owes more to whisky than Islay and there are few blends which do not owe something to an Islay whisky.

Laphroaig

This is the outstanding whisky of Islay. The distillery of Laphroaig is a most attractive place on the sea-shore decorated white with window boxes, and it is not surprising to find that it was run by a lady. The original buildings associated with a farm were built by the Johnstone family in 1815 and it was run by the Johnstones and their descendants till 1954, but in 1950 a limited company had been formed and this came into partnership with Long John in 1962. In the meantime (1923) the capacity of the distillery was doubled by adding two new stills which were replicas of two which had been installed in 1882. Modernised malt barns with the then new type of pagoda kiln were also added and also much-needed new warehouses. Whisky is made in the traditional way.

The strong flavour of Laphroaig is not from the barley for most of this comes from the mainland. What the island has is abundance of rain and acres and acres of peat. Along many of the main roads in Islay peat stacks abound. This peat is no doubt responsible for the taste of the whisky. This is discussed later under 'Peating'. The Islay whiskies are greatly used for blending, and although I have no personal liking for them, I know of many who will drink none other.

The distilleries are spread out round the coast of the island and have to get their barley by sea. Although the men working in them speak English many of the natives still speak Gaelic.

Bruichladdich

It is hard to imagine a distillery on a better site than *Bruichladdich* on the sea-shore looking south across the great bay of the island. If it was nearer centres of industry the area would be worth a fortune. This very small distillery was built in 1881 but was one of the many which went out of production in the bad times. In 1960 it was purchased by A. B. Grant, a blender and exporter of Glasgow, by whom it was completely modernised and its output greatly increased.

Bruichladdich whisky is available only to local publicans, but through the kindness of Mr A. B. Grant I have a bottle. It is a typical Islay whisky with a rich very pleasant flavour but without the medicinal flavour of Laphroaig. It is much used for blending and no doubt goes into the blends 'Bonnie Scot' and 'Special Scot' which are made by the firm, which was bought by Invergordon Distillers in 1972.

Bowmore

Bowmore Distillery may be described as part of the chief town of the island, and although the most central distillery of the island it is on a shelf of the great sea loch Lochindal.

The distillery looks almost like a fortress with an imposing gateway. It was built in 1779 by the Simson family, but in 1880 passed to the brothers Mutter, who were nephews. About the beginning of the century it became the property of Holmes and in 1925 the distillery was bought by J. B. Sherriff & Co., who made many alterations. Indeed it is still known as Sherriff's Bowmore Distillery, but in 1949 it was bought by Grigor, blenders of Inverness, who in 1963 sold it to its present owners, Stanley Morrison Ltd, Glasgow whisky brokers. They have greatly modernised the plant to increase its output, which is now 400,000 gallons annually. The distillery can only make malt for a small proportion of its needs and this no doubt partly accounts for the difference between its whisky and the other Islay malts.

It has a powerful yet delicious almost fruity flavour at 75° proof, quite unlike the other Islay whiskies in that its peatiness is scarcely noticeable, but I understand that this is to be increased to please the blenders. Bowmore whisky is, however, a little difficult to find. In 1970 Stanley Morrison Ltd bought Glengarioch Distillery, at Old Meldrum, Aberdeenshire, from The Distillers Company.

Lagavulin

This is a typical Islay malt but its flavour is not so strong as Laphroaig. The name means the Mill in the Valley, it lies about 3 miles east of Port Ellen. The ruins of Dun-naomhaig Castle stand out nearby on a rocky peninsula. It was a place of note in the twelfth century, when it was a stronghold of the Lords of the Isles. Lagavulin was first mentioned in local records in 1742, when it was nothing more than a series of bothys owned by the Johnstone family, who were engaged in smuggling its products to the mainland. They were succeeded by the Grahams, but in 1835 it became a legal distillery when it was taken over by J. L. Mackie, the uncle of Sir Peter (Restless Peter), the maker of White Horse (see page 69). It is now run in conjunction with Port Ellen Distillery, which has recently been reopened by D.C.L. after being closed for many years. This distillery was built in 1825.

Jura

The first distillery on the nearby island of Jura, famous for its hills known as the Paps, appears to have been built here by James Ferguson & Sons at the end of the seventeenth century. Photographs and records show that it was a substantial place probably capable of making 150,000 gallons, although it is doubtful if it ever did so for, owing to difficulty with the owners of the site, it was closed down about 1904. The present distillery which opened in 1963 is a completely new modern building designed and built by its first managing director, Mr Delmé-Evans for Scottish and Newcastle Breweries. He has since built Glenallachie near Craigellachie for the same company. The island is served by the MacBrayne steamers which visit Islay.

Modern Jura whisky like the old is classed as a 'Highland malt' and is said to be lighter than the Islay malts generally. Its first output is a maturing light flavoured malt which is an eight-year-old of a good single type.

Talisker

The only distillery on the island of Skye is Talisker (D.C.L.). It was begun in 1843 as a private concern and until recently had a relatively small output, but in 1916 it was taken over by The Distillers Company and while the whisky retains its characteristic subtle flavour it is not so mellow as it used to be and it has been darkened. A clear variety is, however, available. It is a light whisky with a distinctly peaty flavour, but not so pronounced as the Islay malts. It is available at the usual 70° and 80° proof and also at 100° proof.

As Mr Gunn says 'at its best it can be superb but I have known it to adopt the uncertainties of the Skye weather'. I find Talisker a little less definitive and distinctive than it used to be. Some do not like its light 'oily-like Irish' flavour—or its variety of peatiness, but I do not find it unpleasant.

Talisker gets its name from a house about 6 miles away from the distillery built for the heir to the Macleods of Dunvegan, the chief landowners of the island. The distillery is in the charming little village of Carbost on the shores of the beautiful Loch Harport. The village lives for the distillery but most of the men also farm small crofts. A visit to the distillery is worth while because it entails a hill drive across the island, noted for its beautiful views of sea lochs and the striking Cuillin hills. At the same time one cannot help wondering why the distillery is there at all except to supply local needs, for all its malt comes to its little jetty by ships which have to go round the north of Scotland and return with cargoes of whisky. There has never been a railway on the island but its bad roads are slowly being modernised.

Highland Park

This famous whisky from Kirkwall in the Orkney Islands deserves a special mention. When I first tasted it at 70° proof, bottled by John Scott, grocer and ironmonger (!), I was a little disappointed, but later when I obtained the 98° or 100° proof I found it entirely different; indeed, it was comparable with the best brandy. Highland Park has always been recognised as one of the best whiskies, no doubt because of the special quality of the Orkney peat, which until the opening of the mosses in Aberdeenshire was commonly transported to distilleries on the mainland—even so far south as Blair Athol. The quality of these peats is discussed later. A 75° proof is supplied by the Wine Society.

This distillery on the hill above the town was established by David Robertson in 1789 on the site of the bothy of the famous smuggler Magnus Eunson. When Robertson died, his brother conveyed the distillery malt barn and other buildings on the site to a Robert Borthwick, who in due course passed it on to his son George. The latter passed it in 1869 to his brother the Reverend James Borthwick. After passing through several hands, including that of the Right Reverend Aeneas Chisholm, Roman Catholic Bishop of Aberdeen, acting as a trustee, it became the sole property of James Grant in 1895, under whose name the company continues. His son Walter and his son-in-law Charles Heydon in 1936 came into the business. On the death of the latter Walter Grant became sole proprietor, but one year later he sold the business to Highland Distilleries, remaining however in charge until he died in 1947. He was succeeded by Mr Patrick Scott as local director.

Kirkwall is the capital of the Orkney Islands. It lies on a beautiful land-locked bay. Its quaint narrow streets and picturesque harbour are steeped in the romance of its ancient Viking association, while the town has many ancient buildings, especially the great cathedral of St Magnus, built by the Norsemen in very early times. Mainland, the chief island, is very agricultural and exports livestock. It is conveniently reached by air from Inverness and by sea from Aberdeen. The distillery does its own malting but the barley is for the most part imported.

Another truly excellent whisky is produced at the smaller nearby distillery of *Scapa* overlooking the famous Scapa Flow. It is of interest that the stills have straight sides. Alas, all this good whisky goes for blending by Hiram Walker. It is a pity it is not available by the bottle.

II. Grain Whisky and Blending

Grain whisky, as we have said, is made for the most part from imported maize in the patent still which is described later. It has not the full flavour of a malt whisky, takes less time to mature and is much cheaper to make. It is not generally drunk as such but is used for blending, that is for mixing with malt whiskies.

Only one grain whisky is available by the bottle. This is *Choice Old Cameron Brig*, which is made by The Distillers Company at the original home of John Haig at Cameronbridge near Windygates in Fife. It is available locally and in Perth. It is preferred by many of the older inhabitants to any other whisky. As it contains the usual amount of alcohol it is sold at the usual price.

I had expected this whisky to be hard and tasteless but it is surprisingly reasonable to drink, especially when well matured. It has a slight malt flavour and is certainly better than no whisky, a little reminiscent of D.Y.C., the Spanish whisky.

It is not generally recognised that maize when chewed has quite a distinctive flavour, indeed, even more than barley and in the making of the whisky about 15 per cent of malted barley is added to the mash to supply the diastase to convert the starch of the maize into maltose, which is also sweet. Before it is sold, 'Cameron Brig' is well matured, although not for such a long time as a good malt whisky. This may not be true of all the grain whisky sold. I have a sample of the grain whisky made at the great distillery at Invergordon and that is quite reasonably good also. It is, however, not yet on the retail market.

Enormous quantities of grain whisky are now being made, not only for the whisky blenders but also for the makers of gin. In addition to the five original distilleries of The Distillers Company at Cameronbridge, Cambus, Carsebridge, Caledonian (Edinburgh) and Port Dundas (Glasgow) great new distilleries have been opened at Dumbarton (Hiram Walker), Airdrie (Inver House*), Girvan (W. Grant), Invergordon (Invergordon Distillers) and Montrose (McNab). Other grain distillers are at Strathclyde (Long John, Seager Evans), Ben Nevis (in Fort William) and North British in Edinburgh. It is of interest that the latter was the first to be built in 1885 in opposition to the newly formed Distillers Company, largely at the instance of Andrew Usher and William Sanderson of Vat 69 fame, in order to secure supplies for the smaller blenders. By the irony of fate both have now joined D.C.L.

After 1860 many grain distilleries were established in mid-Scotland and obviously were a great threat to the Highland distillers, who watched their rivals with apprehension.

Up till that time it had been claimed that the term 'Scotch Whisky' should be confined to pot-distilled whisky made from malted barley; indeed, the manufacture of spirits from corn (then of course by the pot still) had been prohibited in 1795 and 1796. The Highlanders themselves were the first to break with tradition and to import southern barley which they had found was often better for malting. This is generally agreed to-day. Meantime the newly formed Distillers Company had produced from their Cambus distillery a whisky made solely from grain which was quite pleasant to drink and was certainly not unwholesome as had been claimed; in fact, it was better than many immature malts (and many modern blends). Anyone who doubts this can drink 'Choice Old Cameron Brig'.

The question was brought to a head by the 'What is Whisky Case' when in 1905 the Borough of Islington, London, prosecuted several publicans for selling 'an article not of the nature, quality and substance demanded'. This was grain whisky sold as Scotch whisky. As the duty was then negligible it was appreciably cheaper than malt whisky. Evidence was brought that the customers had not been deceived and knew what they were drinking, and the case was not finally decided although it went to the Court of Appeal. The grain distillers were despondent but largely owing to the activities of The Distillers Com-

* A subsidiary of Publicker of Philadelphia, U.S.A.

pany a Royal Commission was set up. The Commission reported in 1909 and concluded:

1. That the name 'whisky' should not be restricted to the product of the pot still.
2. That whisky was a spirit obtained from a mash of cereal grains saccharified by the diastase of malt. That Scotch whisky was whisky as defined above, distilled in Scotland.
3. That since the trade in whisky seems to be honestly and fairly conducted there was no need for special legislation.

This report made grain whisky, Scotch whisky. It also made The Distillers Company. To-day all blended whiskies contain a high proportion of grain whisky, at least 50 per cent but there seems to be little doubt that some inferior blends contain even 80 per cent. No wonder blending is a secret process.

More recently in the Customs and Excise Act of 1952 Scotch whisky is defined as a spirit obtained by distillation in Scotland from a mash of cereal grains saccharified by the diastase of malt and matured in a bonded warehouse in casks for at least three years.

When most people talk of whisky they mean a blend, and most of the whiskies sold in shops are blends, of which there are about two thousand, although there are only just over a hundred malt distilleries. Many brandies, ports, coffees and teas are also blended.

As the name suggests, a blend is a mixture. The blending of whiskies began about 1853 when the firm of Ushers in Edinburgh, who were agents for Smith's Glenlivet whiskies, mixed several, some no doubt better than others, to make Ushers Old Vatted Glenlivet whisky. The idea probably came from the blenders in France who mix especially old and new brandies. Ushers blending, no doubt, added considerably to the amount of Glenlivet whiskies available and produced a more standardised product. Maize was not used until 1865. A few vatted whiskies, that is blends of malts only, are still sold.

Since that time the world of blending has become a world of gimmicks, each company vying with the other to catch the eye.

Shapes of bottles, sizes of bottle, stunt labels and still more posters with catch words have all been part of the advertisement. The popularity of a blend depends largely on salesmanship, and different blends become more popular in one county than in another.

We are all familiar with posters which read 'Don't be vague ask for Haig', 'Johnnie Walker born 1820, still going strong', 'Remove the cork and get the message' (Cutty Sark). There are of course many more.

Nowadays blends invariably contain more than 50 per cent of the cheaper grain whisky, but some contain 60 per cent or even 80 per cent. Most of the whisky flavour comes from malt whiskies of which several dozen may be added. Many blenders boast of the number of malt whiskies in their blends, but what really matters is the quantity and especially the quality of the malt whiskies of which they are made.

In the blending process, the barrels of matured whiskies used are first assembled according to the secret recipe of the blend. Previously the whiskies have been maturing in the bonded warehouses at the distilleries. Each cask is opened and nosed by the blender; only in cases of great doubt is the whisky tasted. It is then closed, rolled over to a long trough, opened again and its contents allowed to flow into the trough, which leads to a huge blending vat where the whiskies are mixed by currents of air. The blended whisky is now 'married' for a year to allow the various whiskies to interact, before it is sold either by the cask or by cases of bottles. Some blenders mix the various malts together first and subsequently add the grain whisky. In modern establishments the bottling process is carried out quite mechanically, but under careful supervision.

Good blending is a very skilled business. The blender of a big company gets his job by his sense of smell, for he has to smell a sample of every whisky used. Each blend has its own secret recipe and the well-known blends try to maintain a remarkable uniformity of standard. Each, too, has developed its own particular clientele. There is no doubt that one can acquire a taste for a particular whisky.

Unfortunately anybody with sufficient capital can set up as a blender and by clever advertising can sell his products—especially if he can keep the price low. With the great demand for whisky the temptation to increase the proportion of immature and grain whisky is very great. Some blends of Scotch whisky are said to contain Irish whiskey but I am assured that by the Act of 1952 this is illegal (see page 5). The latter spelt with an 'e' is, when mature, quite excellent.

When we have said all this about blends we have said the worst. Many are indeed excellent and they can rightly claim to be largely responsible for the modern popularity of whisky. Let us face it, we take whisky for its flavour and the pleasant effects of alcohol, which add to our sense of well-being. Pure alcohol we can buy at a price in a chemist's shop, but it is flavourless. If we take a good blended whisky we get the best of both worlds, a pleasantly flavoured alcohol without the toxic effects which so many malt whiskies produce, especially nausea and headache; but modern malt whiskies when adequately matured are probably not so toxic as the old ones used to be. All this of course depends on the amount which is taken. If we want a little more flavour we can buy for a few shillings more one of the better de luxe whiskies.

Until the advent of the blends, whisky was little drunk in England and then only a few of the light Lowland malts. Brandy and wine were the drinks of the well-to-do. Ale, beer and gin were drunk by most people. At the end of the nineteenth century disease of the vines of France made the supply of wine and brandy difficult to obtain. It was at this time that the French chemist Pasteur (1822–95) began his study of the disease which resulted in the great discovery of bacteria. The enterprising Scots took advantage of the situation and discovered for the English blended whisky. From that moment the blends 'took on' and ever since have retained their place till they have become world sellers. This was largely due to the energy and enterprise of five great firms and personalities, John Haig, John Walker, John Dewar, Buchanan of Black and White and Mackie of White Horse. Each produced blends of the best possible quality and all are now merged into the great Distillers Company Limited.

The standard brands of the big five are remarkably alike and hard to differentiate. White Horse has perhaps most flavour and has a suggestion of Islay whisky, no doubt because of a small content of Lagavulin which the Mackie family owned for many years. Haig has a particularly pleasant double flavour, one of which seems to linger on the palate after it is drunk. How far the just completed distillery at Craigellachie will affect the flavour of 'White Horse' in ten years' time remains to be seen. Generally the darker ones are sweeter. The D.C.L. blends maintain a remarkable standard of quality so that you know what you are getting.

There are of course many other independent blenders producing excellent whiskies but they tend to be very variable. When a company sets out to secure a market in a given area, it naturally sends its very best whiskies, but in many instances it tails off in quality. In the blends it is so much easier to do this than with the pure malts, simply by increasing the relative amounts of grain whisky, new and more mature whiskies. There is little doubt that some of our best blenders have reduced their standard on the excuse that good malts are difficult to get and are expensive.

In addition to the standard blends which normally retail (1971) at about £2·72 a bottle there are the de luxe blends, which are certainly better than the standard blends made by the same houses. Thus Johnnie Walker Black Label is better than Red Label and Dimple Haig better than John Haig Gold Label. They are better because they contain more and better matured malt whiskies and of course cost a few shillings more. Those over 70° proof always cost still more because of the extra taxation on the extra alcohol they contain. Unfortunately the term 'de luxe' is not always on the bottle and the cost is the only indication that the maker considers it 'de luxe'. I have heard it said, by an important distiller, that there is now a demand for de luxe whiskies. This is tantamount to an admission that the public wants a whisky with more flavour.

Unfortunately too the classification is quite arbitrary and is made by the firms themselves, who are never backward in extolling the virtues of their products. In the whisky trade the words 'choice', 'very old,' 'liqueur', 'rare' and the like tend to be used quite indiscriminately and not infrequently the adjective applies more to the label and a fancy bottle than to its contents. Most good whiskies are in quite ordinary bottles but in the whisky trade there are exceptions to everything. Some excellent blends use no superlative adjectives and do not need to. On the other hand, there are blends with exotic names which all are agreed only do discredit to the name whisky. It is of interest that a panel of the Consumers' Association which produces the magazine *Which* found itself unable to distinguish between de luxe and standard whiskies. This does suggest that the difference is not much.

In other words there is nothing for it but to remove the cork and taste the contents, but it is well to remember that a de luxe whisky can easily be made from a good blend simply by adding a little good malt. I like a blend of John Haig two-thirds and Glen Mhor one-third.

In many foreign blends we find whisky at its lowest, although it is not called Scotch. Many have however British names.

They are made from young malts diluted with local spirit made from wheat, oats and rye. They are only fit to be drunk with strong flavouring agents.

Of recent years there have been two interesting developments, the coming in of Americans and Canadians and of the brewers into the field. Both increase the need for production but they do not always improve the quality of blends.

*III. The Blending Houses**

THE DISTILLERS COMPANY LIMITED

The Distillers Company began as an amalgamation in 1877 of six grain distillers to protect their interests. They were John Haig, Cameron Bridge, Fife; M. Macfarlane, Port Dundas, Glasgow; McNab Bros., Glenochil, Menstrie; Robert Moubray, Cambus, Alloa; John Bald, Carsebridge, Alloa; Stewart & Co., Kirkliston, West Lothian. Menzies joined about 1885. Now it is a giant, but it is an amiable giant. In visiting its offices or its distillery managers, often unannounced, nothing but the utmost courtesy has been shown.

The company began with a nominal capital of £2 million and a headquarters in Edinburgh. It became one of the largest companies in the world with a capital of £500 million. It no longer produces plastics and chemicals. Spirits, however, remained by far its greatest interest—accounting for about 80 per cent of the profits, but its interests outside spirits have now been sold to British Petroleum.

D.C.L., as it is conveniently called, was fortunate in being established before the great whisky slump of 1900. Before then whisky appeared to be set for a boom market as it is to-day. Distilleries and blenders sprang up apace until production greatly exceeded demand and many of the newcomers had to go out of business. Notorious amongst these were the Pattison Brothers who had sailed high and too near the wind. When they collapsed, their magnificent warehouses in Leith were bought by D.C.L. for a little more than one-third of their cost of £60,000.

It may be remarked that production in 1898 was a small

* In choosing the companies to be mentioned regard has been taken of quotation on the London Stock Exchange, ownership of distilleries or the making of a blend of special note.

fraction of what it is to-day, but the thirst for whisky has greatly increased all over a parched world! This is indeed an advertisement because its quality has produced the thirst. There are those who to-day hold up a warning finger and suggest that production is again becoming excessive.

Even D.C.L., although it easily weathered the storm of 1898, was not free from difficulties for many were envious of the growth of the giant. The result in 1909 of the 'What is whisky Case' by which grain whisky could be called Scotch Whisky really set the company on the way to fortune (see page 50).

The first world war brought great alarm to the whole whisky industry because the German submarines threatened supplies of food from abroad. There was a feeling that barley, if grown at all instead of wheat, should not be used for making alcohol. Indeed much barley was requisitioned and so little whisky made that there was a shortage for many years after the war had ceased. In 1915 Lloyd George, the Chancellor of the Exchequer, already unpopular for his major increase in the whisky tax of 1909, made a speech praising Russia for reducing the making of vodka and France for suppressing absinthe. Prohibition seemed imminent but was avoided by the brilliant stratagem of James (later Lord) Stevenson of John Walker (see page 65), who was particularly friendly with the Chancellor of the Exchequer, and later Prime Minister, Lloyd George because of his work at the Ministry of Munitions. He suggested that cereals be restricted for whisky making and that no new whisky should be sold till it was three years old. This law did so much good that it has continued ever since, although many would increase the number of years that whisky should be matured. Supplies of yeast for the making of bread were also short, but here The Distillers Company were able to come to the rescue and make the yeast in its distilleries. The company had already in 1899 formed the United Yeast Company to make yeast for its own purposes and for bakeries generally. Complete prohibition was avoided but cereals were rationed to the distilleries and all pot stills closed down for two years and many permanently.

The dire effects which Prohibition (1919–33) was seen later to produce in the United States were also avoided, but the tax on whisky was increased. In 1914 the cost of a bottle of whisky was only 22½p!

It looked as if there might be a scramble for the available stocks and the great amalgamation began. For protection of their own interests in 1915 John Dewar of Perth joined James Buchanan of London, the makers of Black and White. The advantages of this merger became so obvious to the far-seeing genius William H. Ross, the managing director of D.C.L., that eventually in 1925 he, with the greatest tact and perseverance, achieved what had appeared to be the impossible task of bringing into The Distillers Company not only the Buchanan-Dewar combine but also John Walker of Kilmarnock, hitherto great competitors. Thus was born the greater D.C.L. as we know it to-day. Two years later White Horse Distillers, successors to Mackie, was bought and since then the company has gone from strength to strength. In the meantime (1917) D.C.L. had acquired the company of J. & G. Stewart of Edinburgh, who had taken over the whisky blending business of Usher, the original blenders of Edinburgh. Other well-known blenders at first held out but eventually Sandersons of Vat 69 joined in 1937, A. & A. Crawfords in 1944, the much respected firm of J. & W. Hardie, the maker of the de luxe '*The Antiquary*' in 1947. This brought in Benromach distillery in Forres. This excellent blend is now made by Sandersons. Crabbie, a company famed for its ginger wine, came in in 1963.

These amalgamations brought together in the company a large number of malt distilleries and these have since been greatly added to until D.C.L. controls almost half (43) the malt distilleries in Scotland (see page 153), which since 1929 it administers through its subsidiary Scottish Malt Distillers (S.M.D.), whose headquarters is in Elgin. This company actually began as a combination of five Lowland malt distilleries in 1914.

That the company enjoys the confidence of the public is well shown by the fact that as recently as 1959 no less than

£29 million was subscribed by investors for the purpose of providing greater facilities for maturing whisky and for modernising many of its older distilleries. Many of these had been producing over the years famous whiskies under conditions of great difficulty.

Most whiskies of D.C.L. are used for blending but the following are available in bottle: Choice Old Cameron Brig, Talisker, Cardhu, Mortlach, Linkwood, Clynelish, Aultmore,* Rosebank, Glendullan, Ord. The following is a list of its subsidiary companies:

Ainslie & Heilbron (Distillers) Ltd, Baird-Taylor Ltd, John Begg Ltd, Benmore Distillers Ltd, John Bisset & Co. Ltd, Buchanan-Dewar Ltd, James Buchanan & Co. Ltd, Bulloch Lade & Co. Ltd, Crabbie & Son, Cragganmore Distillery Co. Ltd, A. & A. Crawford Ltd, Daniel Crawford & Son, Ltd, Dailuaine-Talisker Distilleries Ltd, Peter Dawson Ltd, John Dewar & Sons Ltd, Distillers Agency Ltd, Distillers Co. (Northern Ireland) Ltd, Donald Fisher Ltd, John Gillon & Co. Ltd, John Haig & Co. Ltd, J. & W. Hardie Ltd, John & Robt. Harvey & Co. Ltd, John Hopkins & Co. Ltd, Low, Robertson & Co. Ltd, W. P. Lowrie & Co. Ltd, D. & J. McCallum Ltd, Macdonald, Greenlees Ltd, John McEwan & Co. Ltd, Macleay Duff (Distillers) Ltd, Mitchell Bros. Ltd, John Robertson & Son Ltd, Wm. Sanderson & Son Ltd, Scottish Malt Distillers Ltd, Slater Rodger & Co. Ltd, J. & G. Stewart Ltd, John Walker & Sons Ltd, James Watson & Co. Ltd, White Horse Distillers Ltd, Gin Distillers & Rectifiers: Boord & Son Ltd, Booth's Distilleries Ltd, Tanqueray Gordon & Co. Ltd. Although many of these companies used to be independent, they no longer have chairmen but only vice-chairmen and managing directors who come under the control of the Committee of Management. The only exception is Lord Forteviot of John Dewar.

The great advantage of the amalgamations is that considerable economies can be effected in the selling of whisky and particularly in the purchase of cereals.

* At the time of writing Aultmore from Keith is not available in London.

The Grain Department of D.C.L. is responsible for buying all grain in use in its distilleries. Unlike many other companies the policy of D.C.L. is to use only home-grown barley for its malts, although it is found that Canadian barley is most suitable for providing the diastase necessary for the fermentation in its five grain distilleries: at Cameronbridge (Windygates), in Fife, Cambus and Carsebridge in Clackmannan, Port Dundas in Glasgow and Caledonian Distillery in Edinburgh. Montrose in Angus has now been converted to malt. These distilleries are under the control of a subsidiary company, Scottish Grain Distillers Ltd, which also is concerned with the production of the important by-product of fermentation, carbon dioxide, used not only for so many aerated waters and beers, but also for ice-creams and as a cooling agent for energy plants. Through a subsidiary, Thomas Borthwick (Glasgow) Ltd, D.C.L. sells by-products of the whisky-making processes (see page 103) for animal feeding stuffs.

The great importance of whisky to the country is that it is a major dollar earner and by its sale we can the more easily buy the food from abroad that we are quite unable to produce for ourselves. The minute of Mr Churchill in 1945 has already been quoted (page 4) and the importance of this statement is just as great to-day as it was thirty years ago: in this D.C.L., by virtue of the volume it produces, plays a leading part. Whisky is one of this country's largest exports, but to achieve this D.C.L. had to ration the home market until 1959 and many say became a little too complacent. During this period many other firms got their feet in the home doors.

The total export of whisky is now over £194 million annually, of which D.C.L. produces about half.

The story of D.C.L. would be incomplete without saying what it has done for the distilleries of Scotland. It is almost possible to say that a distillery may be recognised as one of Scottish Malt Distillers by its clean and tidy appearance which bespeaks efficiency. Too many of the others are very otherwise.

John Haig

As we have seen, the Haig family played a great part in the early days of the patent still and the introduction of grain whisky (see page 110) when they were closely associated with the family of Stein. The Haigs were originally border farmers, the first of whom there is any record being Petrus del Hage, whose name appears in a charter between 1162 and 1166. He appears to have been descended from a Norman knight who came over with the Conqueror in 1066, and was eventually given the lands of Bemersyde which have been in the family of Haig ever since.

The branch of the family which began distilling were farmers in Stirlingshire and, as was usual, distilled as a side-line for the benefit of the family and other friends. Five sons of the early John Haig became distillers, and it is of interest that a sister married John Jameson, the founder of the famous whisky firm of that name in Dublin.

The Haigs were amongst the very first distillers in Scotland and it is recorded that as early as 1655 Robert Haig got into trouble with the local Kirk for working his still on a Sunday.

The Haig brothers and their descendants owned several distilleries in the Lowlands of Scotland, one of the most important being Seggie (at Guardbridge) near St Andrews, of which town William Haig became Provost. His son was the original John Haig who founded the grain distillery at Cameronbridge near the present little town of Windygates in Fife.

The site of the distillery must have been a pleasant wooded dell on the little river but, alas, it is not so now. It is covered by a conglomeration of the dimmest imaginable buildings which speak of the gradual somewhat piecemeal growth of the distillery. The old coach house of John Haig is now incorporated, but it is still recognisable as such. It is hoped that one day, if only for sentimental reasons, the company will rehabilitate the place of its birth.

With the establishment of The Distillers Company in 1877, John Haig became a separate company with headquarters at

Markinch, a few miles distant. Here is now to be seen one of the largest blending and bottling establishments in the world. This company was acquired by The Distillers Company in 1919. At Markinch is blended the famous whisky 'Haig', the standard brand, and the de luxe brand 'Dimple', which stand out amongst whiskies. These whiskies have what I can only call a delicious after-flavour which lingers on the palate and make them now my favourite blend. John Haig has for very many years been the best-selling whisky in the United Kingdom. The company also issues a vatted malt Glenleven, which is a mixture of malts without any grain. It is a disappointing mixture. Over seven hundred different labels in different languages are required for the whiskies.

Another member of the family had also established in Glasgow an export business of Haig and Haig which sold, especially in America, under the brand names of 'Haig and Haig' and 'Pinch'. This firm was badly hit by prohibition in the United States (1919–33), and also joined The Distillers Company in 1923, before becoming a wholly owned subsidiary of John Haig & Co. Ltd, in 1925. It no longer exists as a separate entity and the only Haig remaining as an executive in D.C.L. is a gin distiller in America.

The family of Haig have always been interested in soldiering as well as in whisky, many becoming soldiers of note. Of these, Field Marshal Earl Haig, who led the British Armies to victory during the first world war, was the most outstanding. On retirement he rejoined the company, and was chairman from 1924 until his death in 1928.

John Dewar

John Dewar, the founder of the firm, was born in 1806 and died in 1880. He began as a wine and spirit merchant in the High Street of Perth in 1846 when he was already middle-aged, indeed he was over fifty before he engaged his first traveller. The story of the rise of the House of Dewar is one of slow but sure progression.

At first in 1887 a distillery was rented at Tullymet in southern Perthshire, but in 1896 this was replaced by a new distillery at beautiful Aberfeldy where the River Tay emerges from Loch Tay. By 1923 the firm owned distilleries at Aberfeldy, Lochnagar, Muir of Ord in Ross-shire, Pulteney in Wick with Aultmore, Parkmore and Benrinnes in Banffshire.

To-day Dewar's (called White Label abroad) can be described as a first-class blend with no special characteristics, very like Black and White or Johnnie Walker. Dewar's whisky is after Johnnie Walker's the most popular in the world and is 90 per cent exported. Unlike so many modern blends it never varies because it is based on so many matured malts. It was fortunate to get on the market at the right time and in the right way, for it was the first whisky to be sold by the bottle. Prior to this those wishing to take whisky home took their own jars to the hotel which had a barrel. It is of interest to remark that until Gladstone's Spirit Act of 1860 whisky could not be imported into England in bottles. The necessity to purchase it in eighty-gallon casks was a grave disadvantage. Success was achieved rapidly, for the sons of the original John were men of outstanding ability, not only in business, but in the world of affairs. John Alexander Dewar became Treasurer of the City of Perth and for six years was Lord Provost, but he found time to become a Liberal Member of Parliament for Inverness-shire. As such he was a leader in Scottish affairs, being chairman of two Royal Commissions. In 1907 he was made a baronet and in 1917 raised to the peerage for his splendid services. He became Baron Forteviot of Dupplin in Perthshire—the first of the whisky barons.

Thomas R. Dewar, the younger brother, was even more dynamic and was the super-salesman of the firm, travelling far and wide, and was probably more responsible than anyone else for the success of Scotch whisky in London. He began Dewar's wharf on the Thames where additional bottling was done. It was here on the old Shot Tower that Dewar's Highlander with a waggling kilt in lights advertised it. He became a Sheriff of the City of London and sat as a Conservative Member of

Parliament for St George's in the East. He was knighted in 1902, became a baronet in 1917 and a peer in 1919 as Baron Dewar of Homestall in Sussex. Three times he was Master of the Worshipful Company of Distillers, and was a great personality and wit. One of his famous sayings was 'Do right and fear no man; don't write and fear no woman.' He was a bachelor.

The House of Dewar is rightly proud of the sporting activities of the first Lord Dewar. He took a great practical interest not only in horses but also in dogs. He bred Cameronian which won the Derby after his death in 1930. Dewar was succeeded by P. M. Dewar, who curiously enough was no relation but had worked as a boy in the office. He was chairman from 1930 to 1946. In 1954 the third Lord Forteviot assumed control.

The London headquarters of the firm is the elegant building in the Haymarket built in 1908, and is famous for its pictures, while the new great blending establishment at Inveralmond just north of Perth strikes the eye of everyone who comes from that direction. It occupies forty acres and employs 600 persons. There is no space nor need for the storage of the bottled whisky, which goes as soon as it is in the case. The Chairman each day arrives in a jeep while lesser men arrive by Rolls! Dewar joined with Buchanan in 1915 and in 1925 became part of The Distillers Company. John Dewar, which already holds the Royal Warrant, was given the Queen's Award for Export in 1966. The company also markets a de luxe blend 'Ancestor'.

John Walker

The original John Walker began in Kilmarnock, Ayrshire, as a licensed grocer. Such grocers are very common in Scotland and provide a method by which a lady or her maid can obtain a bottle in the bottom of her grocery basket without being seen coming out of a 'pub'. After various vicissitudes, the worst being when Walker lost all his stock as a result of a flood, slowly but surely he recovered to become a wholesaler and supplier to ships from the great port of Glasgow, and in 1880 opened an office in London. By this time Alexander Walker, a son, controlled the business and he was the real creator in 1908 of 'Johnnie Walker', the blend which is so well known. Previously it had been known as Walker's 'Kilmarnock' whisky. Unfortunately he died nine years later but already he had established his whisky and his company. He was succeeded by his third son Alec and the latter soon had the fortune to be joined by James Stevenson, who was a superb administrator, and between them they built what is now the Johnnie Walker empire, with contacts all over the world and the famous slogan 'Johnnie Walker born 1820, still going strong'. The present firm of John Walker & Sons, Ltd, was formed in 1923 with Sir Alexander Walker as chairman.

During the first war Alec Walker and Stevenson showed their great administrative abilities at the Ministry of Munitions and for his services Walker was knighted, but Stevenson went further, becoming an adviser to the Secretary of State for the Colonies and a member of innumerable Government Committees. He also organised the British Empire Exhibition in 1924. He was given a baronetcy in 1917, a G.C.M.G. in 1922 and in 1924 a peerage, but alas like so many great administrators died at the early age of fifty-three. According to Winston Churchill, 'in ten years of public service he wrote out and consumed the whole of his exceptional strength of mind and body'. There is no longer a Walker as an executive in the company.

The firm of John Walker & Sons acquired a number of distilleries, notably Cardow—pronounced Cardhu—after which a modern single malt, now available, is named. The best blend produced by the firm is Johnnie Walker 'Black Label', well recognised to be a really de luxe whisky. It also markets a standard blend Red Label. Enormous amounts of both are sold abroad, indeed 'Johnnie Walker' remains by far the best-selling brand of Scotch whisky in the world. They are now blended at Barleith to the east of the town but bottling is still done in Kilmarnock.

James Buchanan

The story of James Buchanan and his blend 'Black and White' is fascinating. It is one of the perseverance and energy of one man of great personality worthy indeed of Samuel Smiles's famous book *Self Help*.

He began at the age of fourteen in a shipping office in Glasgow. Here he worked long hours but, soon dissatisfied with his salary, he joined his brother, a grain merchant in that town. By thirty he had seen the road to London like so many Scots and acted as an agent for Charles Mackinlay & Co., whisky merchants and blenders. It is said that he had been refused a partnership in Ainslies of Edinburgh. This was in 1879 but by 1884 he had set up his own firm of James Buchanan & Co., at 61 Basinghall Street, London. His capital was small but he succeeded in obtaining stocks of whisky from his friend W. P. Lowrie in Glasgow, whose firm still runs Convalmore Distillery in Dufftown. Lowrie was one of the first to see the importance of blending and in this vies with Ushers. This distillery was eventually bought by Buchanan and likewise Glentauchers near Keith. Buchanan now controls Dalwhinnie Distillery in Inverness-shire. All are now in D.C.L.

With a keen sense of business and having established a blend, James Buchanan set out to sell it in a big way using all the wiles and stratagems at his command, and he had many. His blend was 'Black and White' from the simple white label on a black bottle. This was registered in 1904. At first the label was Buchanan's blend with 'House of Commons' in larger letters, but this soon vanished when by his energy he had established himself and his blend 'Black and White' became popular and known as such.

In 1898 James Buchanan bought the Black Swan Distillery in Holborn, a famous coaching inn, and this he rebuilt. From here, since I remember, came loads of whisky in the handsome drays drawn by wonderful horses with immaculate drivers in picturesque stage-coach uniforms. This really was an advertisement which everyone admired. Alas they have been replaced in London by motor vans, but the drays continue in Glasgow.

Pictures of James Buchanan show him to have been a tall spare man of distinguished aristocratic appearance, turned out almost as a dandy in the best Victorian manner. Like the Dewars he loved horses. When his fortunes flourished he became a successful race-horse owner and twice won the Derby. In 1920 he became a baronet and in 1922 was raised to the peerage as Lord Woolavington of Lavington, but he never lost the personal touch nor his willingness to help anyone whom he thought worked really hard and was worthy of assistance. (I had personal knowledge of this.) He died much mourned in 1935 at the age of eighty-six, but his company flourishes.

The headquarters of the firm was in 1953 moved to Devonshire House, Piccadilly, on the site of the mansion of that name which became so famous for its parties in the last century when it belonged to the Duke of Devonshire. For long Buchanan had stood apart from The Distillers Company but in 1915 amalgamated with Dewars and both joined the great company in 1925.

During the second world war, and until 1959, in common with most Scotch whiskies 'Black and White' was in short supply, but now this excellent blend is freely available. However, the demand has become so great that an entirely new blending and bottling plant, capable of bottling 4,600 dozen bottles an hour, has been built at Stepps in the north-eastern outskirts of Glasgow. 'Black and White' with 'Vat 69' dominate the German market. The company also markets 'Buchanan's De Luxe'. This is certainly one of the best blends and deserves to be better known. More recently the company, owing to the renewed interest over the last few years in malt whiskies, has marketed 'Strathconon', a twelve-year-old blend of Highland malts which has the same underlying flavour as Buchanan's. Both are delicious.

WHITE HORSE

The name 'White Horse' comes from an ancient inn in the Canongate of Edinburgh where it is said the officers of Prince Charlie used to relax during the rebellion of 1745, but white horses have long been a traditional symbol of victory. From the White Horse Cellar in Edinburgh set out at five in the morning, every Monday and Friday, the stage coach to London, 'which performs the whole journey in eight days (if God permits)' (*February* 1754). There is however doubt as to whether the whisky has any real connection with this. It is made in Glasgow. The founder of the firm was James Logan Mackie, one of the few heads of firms who was actually trained as a distiller in Islay. It was he who saw the advantages in the name, but it was his nephew Peter Mackie, nicknamed 'restless Peter', who really made the firm of Mackie & Co. The malt part of the blend was largely from two distilleries which still flourish; that at Craigellachie, bought in 1915, overlooking the valley of the Spey, which has recently been largely reconstructed, and Lagavulin on the island of Islay which give the whisky its slightly unusual flavour. This he took over in 1888. By the outbreak of the first war 'White Horse' was the drink of innumerable army messes; indeed, I well remember filling R.A.M.C. panniers with it to take on service in 1915.

Peter Mackie was an ardent politician on the Unionist side but nevertheless was made a baronet by Lloyd George's Coalition Government in 1920. He died in 1924 at the age of sixty-nine leaving behind him a whisky which, by his great drive and in spite of great competition, he had made famous throughout the world. The 'White Horse' of to-day is, however, a much less peaty whisky than some of its predecessors of thirty years ago, which it was claimed on the label were based on a recipe of 1746 when there could not have been blends in the modern sense. Blended whiskies are now much more standardised but 'White Horse' still stands out as a blend with flavour. It leads the field in South Africa.

In 1924 the name of the company became White Horse

Distillers Limited, which has its headquarters in St Vincent Street, Glasgow. In 1927 White Horse joined The Distillers Company to complete the amalgamation of the Big Five. It was the first firm to introduce screw-top caps to the whisky bottles, and only recently a bottle with a special grip to make it more easily held. White Horse also makes the special blend Laird of Logan's which is excellent.

William Sanderson

Vat 69 made by Sanderson is one of the most popular whiskies, especially with the ladies. It is pleasantly sweet, not too smokey. The story of its introduction is interesting. William Sanderson, a maker of alcoholic cordials in Leith, decided to produce a new blend of whiskies at the time when blend-making was the thing to do. He made up a hundred vattings and asked his more knowledgeable friends to express their opinion on them. The verdict was unanimous and 69 was the number of the cask. This also was Sanderson's own preference and so it all began in 1882. It is recorded that William Sanderson paid particular attention to the valued advice of an author friend. It is advice that many modern blenders should take to heart.

> William Sanderson noted:
> No spirit can pay better for bonding than whisky, the first outlay averaging from two shillings to three shillings a gallon(!) is very little and the improvement by age is far superior to the trifling interest on the first cost. Nothing tends more to increase the reputation of a spirit merchant than supplying good and well matured spirit. The distiller whose outlay is large for casks will be inclined to give better terms to the merchant who will find his own casks and it is well known that whisky stored in sherry casks soon acquires a mellow softness which it does not get when put into new casks; in fact the latter if not well seasoned will impart a *woodiness* much condemned by the practised palate.

In sherry casks the spirit like-wise acquires a pleasing tinge of colour which is much sought for.

This was written by William Sanderson in 1864 twenty years before Vat 69 was born, and how true it is today, when so many blenders sell their products long before they are mature.

'Quality tells' was the slogan attached to Vat 69 and this was really true of the whisky, for in it was whisky from Royal Lochnagar. This is a little farm-like distillery above Balmoral Castle on Deeside. Sanderson had long been a friend of the proprietor John Begg (see page 73), and when the latter died he became a director.

In 1884 Sanderson became the owner of Glengarioch Distillery at Old Meldrum, which is at the centre of the great barley-growing plain of Aberdeenshire. This assured him of further supplies of malt whisky, but with the establishment of The Distillers Company in 1877 he had become doubtful about supplies of grain whisky. The result was the formation of a new company with a strong board of blenders with Andrew Usher as chairman and including Bell of Perth. A new distillery, 'The North British', using the 'patent still' was built at Gorgie in Edinburgh and still operates in, of course, a modernised form, but times change, for in 1937 the firm of William Sanderson & Sons became part of The Distillers Company. The company received the Queen's Award for Exports in 1967.

In the meantime (1935) the firm amalgamated with Booth's Distilleries and this brought into the group three more distilleries: Royal Brackla near Nairn, Millburn at Inverness and Stromness in the Orkney Islands. The latter, which was very small, no longer operates.

Royal Brackla also continues as a D.C.L. distillery. This had been established in 1812 by Captain William Fraser on ground leased from the fifth Earl and twenty-third Thane of Cawdor. It is now leased by Bisset, and had the distinction of being the first distillery to be awarded the Royal prefix, which was given by King William IV, who admired its whisky so much.

Control of the firm of Sanderson passed from father to son for three generations and it maintains its independence as one of the Big Six of D.C.L. It still has a headquarters at South Queensferry and offices in Stanhope Gate near Hyde Park in London. The popularity of Vat 69 with the seal of the Sanderson family, the Talbot Hound and the motto *Sans Dieu Rien* is unabated.

In *The Lancet*, 1907, i. 884, the following authoritative statement appeared, and was given on the bottles. This has however been discontinued.

> In view of the statements frequently made as to present medical opinion regarding alcohol and alcoholic beverages we the undersigned think it desirable to issue the following statement, a statement which we believe represents the teaching of leading clinical teachers as well as that of the great majority of medical practitioners.
>
> Recognising that in prescribing alcohol the requirement of the individual must be the governing rule, we are convinced of the correctness of the opinion so long and generally held that alcohol is a rapid and trustworthy restorative. In many cases it can be truly said to be truly life saving owing to its power to sustain cardiac and nervous energy while protecting the wasting nitrogenous tissues. As an article of diet we hold the universal belief of civilised mankind that the moderate use of alcoholic beverages is for adults usually beneficial, amply justified.
>
> We deplore the evils arising from the use of alcoholic beverages. But it is obvious that there is nothing however beneficial which does not in excess become injurious.

The statement was signed by sixteen eminent men including the Professor of Medicine in Glasgow, Sir William Gowers, the famous London neurologist, Sir Thomas Fraser, Professor of Materia Medica and Clinical Medicine in Edinburgh, and the Professor of Physiology at King's College London, my predecessor!

Sandersons now make the excellent de luxe whisky 'The

Antiquary' but put it up in a fancy bottle which I feel sure the late Mr Hardie whom I knew, would not have approved of. The whisky does not need it!

John Begg

This whisky, now a blend, but originally a malt, was made at the charming little distillery on the hillside above Balmoral Castle on Deeside, Aberdeenshire. John Begg was one of those who took advantage of the act of 1823 to build a distillery which he called Lochnagar after the adjoining mountain. Byron, who had spent much of his boyhood in the area, wrote:

> England: Thy beauties are tame and domestic
> To one who has roved o'er the mountains afar
> Oh for the crags that are wild and majestic
> The steep frowning glories of dark Loch-na-Gar.

John Begg was luckier than his colleague of Deeside who had his new distillery near Banks o' Dee burnt down, so violent was the reaction of the 'smugglers' against the legal distillers.

It is recorded that Queen Victoria with Prince Albert, her Consort, and some of their family visited the distillery some three days after they arrived at Balmoral in 1848 and sampled its product. This visit no doubt contributed to permission being given for the use of the prefix 'Royal', only given previously to Royal Brackla.

Royal Lochnagar is indeed a wonderful whisky with a subtle flavour of sherry from the cask in which it has been matured—a flavour which cannot be imitated by putting a little sherry in any whisky. It is a privilege to have tasted such a rich whisky. It is not generally available. Perhaps it is kept at the distillery in case the present Queen and her Consort pay a call, but there is not enough of it made to justify a single bottling. At one time it was the most expensive whisky in Scotland. It is of course rated first-class for blending and in this regard has been specially associated with William Sanderson, the maker of Vat 69, but the name of John Begg is perpetuated as 'J.B. Blue Cap' and as the de luxe blend 'J.B. Gold Cap'. John Begg became a subsidiary of D.C.L. in 1916.

Bulloch Lade

This company owns the picturesque little distillery of Caol Ila on the water's edge on the north-east coast of Islay. It is tucked in at the bottom of an escarpment where it has its own little jetty to and from which the Scottish Malt Distillers' boat sails regularly. The company was formed in 1856 when Lade & Co. joined Bulloch & Co., who had previously traded separately and owned Loch Katrine Distillery near Glasgow and Lossit Distillery in Islay. In 1857, they took over Caol Ila and in 1858 the now defunct distillery Benmore in Campbeltown. The company, which has its headquarters at 75 Hope Street, Glasgow C2, became a subsidiary of D.C.L. in 1927. It produces Bulloch Lade 'Gold Label' and a de luxe brand 'Old Rarity,' a light blend at 75° proof which is one of the very popular light whiskies.

A. & A. Crawford

This is another Leith blending firm which like Sandersons made its name by producing a good blend, Crawford's 'Three Star', and later in the 1920's the de luxe 'Five Star' which has an increasingly good reputation. It is 'one of the good things in life'.

The firm began in 1860 when the brothers Archibald and Aikman Crawford set up business near Sandersons at 8 Quality Lane, Leith. When they died, in 1880 and 1885 respectively, a Mr David Ireland became the senior partner and he was entrusted with the training of the two sons of the original partners, Archie and Harry. The present 'Three Star' label was probably designed in 1900.

After the first war, during which Harry was awarded the M.C. as a major in the Royal Scots, there was great expansion and Crawford's whisky became widely known at home and abroad. Crawford's moved to 93 Constitution Street. Harry after a period of ill-health died in 1928 and Archie in 1937, but in the meantime Mr. W. W. Winton had come into the firm and he was left as sole director. A family company, A. & A. Crawford, was formed in 1942 but sold out to D.C.L. in 1944.

The Distillers Agency

This company began as the export division of The Distillers Company but became separated when the great amalgamations were beginning. Since then it has acquired two Speyside distilleries, Knockdhu and Speyburn. The former was the first distillery built by D.C.L. The company is responsible for the production and export of the well known and popular blend 'George IV', the lesser known 'Highland Nectar' and the de luxe blend 'George IV Supreme'. It bottles also the Lowland malt Rosebank, which is made nearby at Falkirk. The headquarters of the company is at South Queensferry just by the great Forth Bridges.

D. & J. McCallum

This is again an old Edinburgh firm founded in 1807 by the brothers Duncan and John McCallum. Their small inn known colloquially as the Tattie Pit was for long a favourite rendezvous of the Edinburgh worthies of the day, and the blend 'Perfection' Scots whisky has from small beginnings gradually made itself known throughout the world. The firm increased its activities by moving to Gibbs Entry on the opposite side of the street, but these premises were utterly destroyed in the isolated German air-raid on Edinburgh in 1916. Now it occupies the beautiful house in 4 Picardy Place well known for its interior decoration and fireplaces by one of the Adam brothers.

This excellent blend which is best known as simply 'McCallum's' is marketed in a distinctive flask-shaped bottle with the name Scots instead of Scotch whisky. The de luxe McCallum which is distinctly peaty is particularly good. McCallum became a fully owned subsidiary of D.C.L. in 1953, and in that year Glenlochy Distillery at Fort William just below Ben Nevis was purchased.

John McEwan

'Abbots Choice' is perhaps not in the highest flight as a flavoured whisky but it has many admirers.

John McEwan who originated it was an enterprising farmer from Perthshire who from time to time brought his animals to the Edinburgh market. The story goes that on one such visit he lost his dogs and wandered into a tavern to look for them. One excuse is as good as another! Discovering that the whisky trade was booming he decided to enter it. He invented a blend which he called 'Abbots Choice' and bought Linkwood Distillery on the outskirts of Elgin. He also bought or opened various licensed premises from which to sell his blend. Distilling is said to have been done at Linkwood since 1790, although of course the small distillery has been much modernised—most recently in 1964 by D.C.L. who had bought John McEwan in 1933. Apart from the blend to which it contributes Linkwood produces a simple but good malt whisky (see page 76).

J. & G. Stewart

This company as it now is incorporates two other old Edinburgh businesses, Andrew Usher & Co. and James Gray & Sons.

James Stewart began in 1779 as a tea and wine merchant. It is to be noted that the contacts between France and Scotland during the Stuart period had made French wines very popular. His sons John and George, however, greatly developed the business, especially an export trade with Sweden, but after their deaths it passed through several hands and eventually became a limited company in 1899.

J. & G. Stewart

Stewarts own North Port Distillery in the ancient city of Brechin in Forfarshire, an old distillery on such a steep hillside that gravity provides most of the power.

James Gray began in the Canongate, also as a wine and spirit business, and this was owned by the family until 1889, when it was bought by a William Menelaws. Under his guidance a considerable export trade with the colonies grew up, but after his death his son sold the business to The Distillers Company in 1918.

Andrew Usher—like Gray, a border man—founded his business in 1813, first in Meadow Place, moved to Wharton Place near Lothian Street and in 1823 to West Nicholson Street, where the headquarters of J. & G. Stewart were until they moved to Maritime Street, Leith, in 1970.

Usher owned the Edinburgh Distillery from 1860 and is to be remembered in the trade as one of those who with William Sanderson opposed The Distillers Company by building in 1887 the North British Distillery for making grain whisky. He became the first chairman and Sanderson the first managing director (see page 71).

The firm of Usher had early established a connection with the Smiths of Glenlivet and were the pioneers of blending, which as we have already noted was so greatly responsible for the popularity of modern whisky. Two of the first Andrew's sons in the business were noble benefactors of their native city of Edinburgh. Andrew is well remembered as the donor of the great Usher Hall in Lothian Road where concerts and the like are held, while John gave the Usher Institute of Public Health in Warrender Park Road and endowed the first chair in the subject in Britain. He retired in 1910 and was granted a baronetcy. Two other brothers went into the beer business and developed the Park Brewery.

The blends marketed by J. & G. Stewart are 'Jamie Stuart', 'Green Stripe' and of course the excellent 'Usher's Old Vatted Glenlivet', which is difficult to find outside Edinburgh but deserves to be better known. They also have the de luxe whiskies 'Antique Jamie Stuart' and 'Usher's Extra'. Why the firm troubles to market so many I really do not understand, but it does suggest that each has its clientele. Stewart's have the Royal Warrant granted to Usher's in 1912, and became part of D.C.L. in 1919. At that time Usher's had four million gallons of whisky in bond, which was invaluable to the other members of the company at the time when good whisky was scarce.

Benrinnes and Dailuaine-Imperial

In addition to the distilleries associated with the well-known whiskies there are many which make malt whiskies for the trade. Benrinnes and Dailuaine-Imperial are two belonging to D.C.L. in the Speyside area. They have been developed from old farms but are now great factories which supply good honest whiskies of not great distinction but in enormous quantities for blending.

OTHER BLENDERS

The Distillers Company has not had a monopoly of the lucrative field of blending; indeed, it only produces about one-half of the blended whisky made. Even at an early stage there was considerable opposition (see William Sanderson). Of recent years because of the popularity of whisky there has been great competition amongst the blenders, and this has certainly been increased by the building of the great grain distilleries at Invergordon, Dumbarton, Girvan and Airdrie. Some of the blenders own malt distilleries, but others rely entirely on what they are able to purchase. In this it should be said that The Distillers Company has shown great generosity and even supplies its competitors. Several firms from the United States and Canada have now come in to share the spoils and have purchased malt distilleries.

The largest or best known of these firms are described and given in alphabetical order, but there are many small blenders which produce excellent whiskies. Several alas also produce blends of immature malts with a high proportion of the cheaper grain whisky, while some distilleries allow more 'foreshots' than others. If too much of the latter is allowed whisky tends to become cloudy when water is added like arak or absinthe. These blends naturally give whisky a bad name abroad. At home they eliminate themselves but abroad they create a very difficult problem, the more so because some merchants abroad are not beyond falsifying the labels and a trade in empty bottles exists. Some blenders with a large export trade use special bottles which cannot be refilled.

Arthur Bell

The firm of Arthur Bell & Sons of Perth was founded in the year 1825 by T. R. Sandeman, who opened a small shop near to the ancient Kirk of St John and traded as a whisky merchant. In due course he was joined by James Roy and in 1851 Arthur Bell entered the firm. By the year 1865 Arthur Bell controlled the business and in 1895 when he took into partnership his two sons the firm became known as Arthur Bell & Sons.

The original Bell died in 1900 and he was succeeded by Arthur Kinmont Bell who, when the firm was converted to a limited company in 1922, became Chairman and Managing Director. Since 1942 when A. K. Bell died there has not been a Bell on the Board of the company, but the name is well remembered through his philanthropic work. It was he who established the Gannochy Trust which has done so much to improve the amenities of the city and the welfare of its elder citizens. In recognition of his work on behalf of others he was made a Freeman of the city in 1938.

The firm grew up at the end of the nineteenth century as small blenders supplying local needs and had to purchase whiskies where it could. After the depression of the early 1930's, when so many distilleries went into the doldrums and changed hands, Bell's bought three distilleries, Blair Athol at Pitlochry and the Dufftown-Glenlivet Distillery, Dufftown, both in 1933 from Peter Mackenzie & Co., and in 1936 they purchased Inchgower Distillery near Fochabers which had been run by the Wilson family since it was built in 1871.

Blair Athol, which is at the southern outskirts of Pitlochry in Perthshire, was established as a legal distillery in the year 1825, and Dufftown-Glenlivet was built in 1887.

All three distilleries have been greatly modernised and with them the company is assured of supplies of good malt whiskies which are no doubt responsible for the excellent reputation of Bell's blends. Inchgower, Blair Athol and Dufftown which are available as single malts have already been described. A better Bell's, a de luxe whisky known as 'The Golden Bell', has now been issued 'because the demand is for de luxe whiskies'.

The firm now has blending and bottling establishments in Edinburgh and Perth with warehouses at Auchtermuchty in Fife, and Halbeath near Dunfermline. The company in 1967 opened a new blending and bottling plant at East Mains, West Lothian and another at Dunfermline.

Berry Bros. & Rudd

'Remove the cork and get the message' says 'Cutty Sark'. The name is that of the famous tea clipper, 'the last and greatest survivor of the lovely sailing ships which brought credit and renown to the ship builders and seafaring men of these islands', said the Duke of Edinburgh. He is president of the *Cutty Sark* Preservation Society which is responsible for the old ship now for ever on show at Greenwich. She was called after the witch in Burns's poem 'Tam O'Shanter' who wore a short shirt—a cutty sark in Scots dialect—and became the figure-head of the ship.*

The name was given by Francis Berry of Berry Bros. after what was no doubt an excellent lunch to James McBey, the Scots artist who suggested the name and designed the present label. It is to be noted that the correct adjective Scots is used not Scotch.

This was in 1933 when the enterprising Berry & Rudd were preparing a new blend specially for the American market at the end of Prohibition. The story goes that just before drinking again became legal in the United States a few bottles of 'Cutty Sark' had found their way into the rum runners' havens in Canada and the West Indies and had been approved of by two men, Charlie Guttman, a former Prohibition Enforcement Officer, and John Culhane, an Irishman in the property business. They made up their minds that after ten years of bootleg 'hooch', Americans couldn't take real Scotch and needed a light whisky, light in colour and flavour but with normal strength. On getting 'Cutty Sark' they set up what is now the great Buckingham Corporation to sell the whisky on a large scale. This corporation is now controlled by Schenley which also controls 75 per cent of Seager Evans (see page 89). Schenley itself is now owned by Glen Alder of New York.

* The figure-head of the reconditioned ship is more adequately clothed.

Guttman eventually went on his own to found the Paddington Corporation which sells 'J. & B. Rare' (see page 88).

'Cutty Sark' is a light coloured blend which appeals not only to the American market, but to others who like their whisky neat. It has a delicate taste reminiscent of the brandy-like flavour of old Lowland malt.

It is bottled at 70° proof, but at 75° proof for the export market.

The firm of Berry Bros. began when George Berry, who had come up from Exeter in 1803, took control of the firm of his grandfather, John Clark, at No. 3 St James's Street, within sight of St James's Palace. Ever since, the family of Berry, which is described as being very philoprogenitive, has been connected with it. Hugh Rudd joined the firm in 1920 after leaving the army. He belonged to an old East Anglian family which had a wine business in Norwich and an intimate knowledge of the Continent and its vineyards. He brought the new blood necessary for the development of the business, but the name did not appear in the title of the firm until it became a limited company in 1940.

No. 3 St James's Street had been the haunt of fashion during the whole of the nineteenth century and apart from the excellency of its wines was well known for the scales and the records it kept of the weights of famous personages, including that of the Duke of Wellington and King William IV. The firm had been of note in the wine trade for two centuries, indeed the present buildings were built for William Pickering in 1731, but it was not till 'Cutty Sark' appeared that the world of whisky took notice.

Warner Allen's book on No. 3 not only gives the story of the firm but sheds an interesting light on what was a most fascinating period of London's social history.

Matthew Gloag

The firm of Matthew Gloag & Son and its 'Grouse' whisky deserves mention because it is one of the sturdy small concerns which for a long time has been producing a delicious slightly peaty whisky in very limited quantity. It is obviously blended from well-matured malts.

Matthew Gloag began in modest premises in Perth in 1814 when the use of whisky was limited to Scotland, but it is slowly getting grander. The firm, which is also an importer of wines, is remarkable because the business went from father to son for five generations of the same name, but in 1970 the company was bought by Highland Distilleries. It relies on no gimmicks, but a good name. The brochure of the firm contains what is perhaps the best boost for whisky:

> Scotsmen the world over use it, neat to warm them when cold, diluted to refresh them when warm, to revive them when exhausted, as a medicine in sickness, as an aid to digestion, as a sedative for sleeplessness, and, universally, to celebrate the meeting with, or parting with, friends, confident that, used in moderation, it will suit the occasion as nothing else will do, and with nothing but good effect. Millions of men in every clime have found that these Scotsmen are right.

The whisky, like the sentence, is a good mouthful!

Highland Distilleries

This company was formed in 1887 to acquire the Islay Distillery Company of William Grant & Co. with Bunnahabhain Distillery, built in 1881, and the Glenrothes Glenlivet Distillery, built in 1878. The company chairman was Mr W. A. Robertson, who founded about 1862 the small wholesale wines house in Glasgow of Robertson & Baxter.

The Highland Distilleries Company, Ltd, now owns six distilleries, and these include Tamdhu Glenlivet, where the Saladin method of malting is used, and Glenglassaugh Distillery near Banff. This had been erected in 1876, and in 1964 was almost entirely re-built and is now one of the best designed distilleries in the country. In 1935 Highland Park distillery,

Orkney, was purchased. This was one of the earliest licensed distilleries, and produces a distinctive single malt whisky of high quality (see page 47). In 1965 the company began construction of a large new warehouse at Buckley, near Bishopbriggs, Lanarkshire. The Highland Distilleries Company, Ltd, is a public company with a capital of about two and a half million pounds. Robertson & Baxter, Ltd, now Scotch Whisky Blenders and Merchants, act as its sole agents, and Highland Distilleries has a 35·4 per cent interest. The two companies are closely associated and occupy the same building in West Nile Street, Glasgow, where a laboratory for testing samples is maintained.

Robertson & Baxter, Ltd, are blenders to the Trade, and are proprietors of such Scotch Whisky as 'Red Hackle' (Hepburn & Ross, Ltd), 'Scottish Cream' (Kinloch Distillery Co. Ltd), 'Lang's Old Scotch Whisky' (Lang Bros. Ltd) (see Glengoyne). They also provide supplies of blended whisky for Berry Bros. & Rudd (see page 81) for 'Cutty Sark' Scotch Whisky.

Hill Thomson

This is a typical Edinburgh firm which has marketed its well-known 'Queen Anne' blend for many years, although of course it has no historical association with the Stuart Queen. It was begun in 1793 when William Hill set himself up in Rose Street Lane, but he rapidly became so successful that he moved to the better address in Frederick Street. In 1857 William Thomson joined Hill and the firm acquired its present name. The popularity of 'Queen Anne' is, however, credited to William Shaw, who came on the scene in 1883, and the name of Shaw still appears four times in the list of directors.

In 1936 a limited company was formed and this became public in 1946 but in 1970 the company which had a 26·8 per cent interest in Longmorn, joined the Glen Grant–Glenlivet combine. Hill Thomson received the Royal Warrant in 1838 from Queen Victoria and has been a recognised purveyor to Royalty ever since.

'Queen Anne' is a first-class blend with a slightly peaty flavour. It incorporates eighteen whiskies, most of which are from Speyside. The company also produces a de luxe whisky 'Something Special', a rich pleasantly peaty blend, but alas it is marketed in a bottle more reminiscent of scent than a good whisky which is really worthy of a better name. (See also Longmorn.)

Macdonald & Muir

This is again a firm of Leith blenders who not only make the well-known 'Highland Queen', standard, 'Grand 15' and Martins V.V.O., but also run two distilleries, Glenmorangie at Tain in Cromarty which was established in 1843, and Glen Moray at Elgin which had been built in 1897. The malt whisky of Glenmorangie has already been described (page 33), that from Glen Moray goes entirely for blending.

The original firm of Macdonald & Muir was begun in 1893 by Mr Roderick Macdonald and Mr Alexander Muir, who had been 'bred to the trade'. It is now a subsidiary of Macdonald & Martin.

They built up a business at 3 Kirkgate so rapidly that in 1902 they were able to move to their present site at Queen's Dock, Leith. In addition to the distilleries the company, which was incorporated in 1936, has five large bonded warehouses for maturing, blending and bottling. The company also owns Muirheads, the well-known spirit merchants in George Street, Edinburgh, where an extremely good display of malt whiskies is to be seen.

Mackinlay & McPherson

Mackinlay-McPherson's origins go back to 1815, when a John Hunter set up a wine business in Edinburgh to which Charles Mackinlay was apprenticed. Mackinlay showed his ability so rapidly that when the business under another name was transferred to Leith he soon became a partner and later sole proprietor. Later he became a figure noted for his public services. Five generations of Mackinlay helped to build up the family firm and an idea of its early standing is indicated by the fact that one of the great pioneers of blending, James Buchanan (q.v.), was with the firm before he established his own.

For fifty years the company was controlled by three families, Mackinlays, Watsons and Thomsons, but in 1961 it was sold out to Scottish and Newcastle Breweries (see below), who entered the Scotch whisky trade in 1952 when, as William McEwan, they purchased the old-established family firm of John E. McPherson of Newcastle-upon-Tyne, which had been founded by the McPherson family in 1856 and had established themselves as whisky blenders of repute, receiving the Royal Warrant from King George V. The amalgamation of Mackinlay and McPherson with the establishment of a modern and large new blending and bottling plant in Leith added greatly to the facilities for the blending and bottling of their increasingly popular brands.

In 1892 James Mackinlay in association with John Birnie had built Glen Mhor Distillery in Inverness, and later acquired the nearby Glen Albyn Distillery. The excellent Glen Mhor has already been described. Four blends are now marketed, 'Mackinlay's', a full-bodied traditional whisky, and 'Legacy', a de luxe blend which is slightly lighter. Under the McPherson label appear 'Cluny', a standard light blend, and a de luxe variety at twelve years old. Both Mackinlay's and Cluny enjoy a thriving world export trade and Cluny is particularly popular in the United States.

The Scottish and Newcastle Breweries was formed by a series of amalgamations which began when the two Edinburgh brewing firms, William Younger, which had been founded in 1749, and William McEwan, founded in 1856, joined together in 1931 to form Scottish Brewers. Newcastle breweries, which had already bought McPhersons in 1952, came in in 1960 and the new group bought Mackinlay in 1961.

This enterprising company has since built distilleries in the Island of Jura and at Glenallachie near Aberlour, and so has a supply of excellent malts for its blends with which to supply its almost 2,000 tied houses. It also has an interest in the great sporting centre at Aviemore.

International Distillers & Vintners

This is a comparatively new group formed in 1962. It consists of four principal firms, W. & A. Gilbey, whose whisky 'Spey Royal' is an excellent blend; Gilbey Twiss, who handle the wholesale distribution of Smirnoff Vodka and Hennessy's brandy in this country; Justerini & Brooks, the London wine merchants, who give their name to 'J. & B. Rare'; and the old company of United Vintners who operate nearly 400 retail shops in Britain under the Peter Dominic label.

The modern romance of Peter Dominic is one which should be recorded. This is the name of the firm made by Paul Dauthieu, of French parents, who began work as a humble waiter during the twenties in London. He flitted from one job to another until he became salesman to a firm of London wine merchants. The advent of the war caused Paul to get the sack and £100, with which he opened a modest shop in Horsham. When he joined the R.A.F. his wife ran the business, which after a period of stress became so successful that by 1959 sixteen shops where wines and spirits were sold at reasonable prices had been opened in adjoining towns.

In 1963 the business, which had grown to 21 shops, was sold to I.D.V. for three-quarters of a million pounds, but alas Paul Dauthieu died of cancer five years later, when he was about to retire.

Gilbey's also operate subsidiaries which distribute in Canada, South Africa and Australia. The combine controls, through Gilbey, three Speyside distilleries, Glen Spey, Strathmill and Knockando, and utilises a large new bond at Strathleven which is entirely concerned with the blending and bottling of 'J. & B. Rare'. It also markets two whiskies, 'Catto's Rare Highland',

'Cameron's Shooting Lodge', and such well-known products as Gilbey's Gin and Dry Monopole champagne.

Justerini & Brooks is one of the oldest established wine merchants in London and has had the Royal Warrant for nine successive reigns. The firm was established by a love-sick Italian, Giacomo Justerini of Bologna, who followed an opera singer, Signorina Belloni, to London in 1749. He brought with him the jealously guarded recipes of his uncle—a distiller in Bologna—for the making of remarkably palatable liqueurs. Fortunately he met through the good offices of the lady a Samuel Johnson, not the famous doctor, already established as an actor, dramatist and producer, and especially his nephew George Johnson, who was prepared to finance the setting up of premises in Pall Mall, the haunt of quality some ninety years before Trafalgar Square was cleared for Nelson's Column. Justerini made up the recipes and carried out the distilling. Johnson was responsible for the office. Unfortunately Mr Johnson was killed when a runaway horse overturned his sedan chair and his son preferred to sell his share in the business. It was bought in 1831 by a Mr Brooks, a gentleman of fashion. It is recorded that the grounds of his house in St John's Wood were large enough to include a snipe shoot. This began a new era for Justerini & Brooks, who have gone from strength to strength now with premises in St James's Street, and in Hatton Garden.

In addition to its own 'J. & B. Rare', the firm controls the sales of the famous blend 'Old Mathew' of Chalié, Richards & Co., and like so many wine merchants has its own brand 'J. & B. Club'.

Gilbey's have also an interesting history. They were and still are 'Merchants of wine', importers of clarets, sherry and ports. The real founders were Walter and Alfred Gilbey, who had returned from the Crimean War without occupation or assets. In 1857 with the assistance of an older brother, they established a wine business at the corner of Berwick Street and Oxford Street, but later acquired the famous Pantheon in Oxford Street, which had been the place of entertainment of fashion.

They also began to distil gin. This was more important than appeared at the time because they developed in the U.S.A., and Gilbey's 'London Gin' was ready for the cocktail boom in the 1920's.

In 1887, the year of Queen Victoria's Jubilee, the Gilbeys saw that the phylloxera disease of the vines in France and Spain was certainly going to affect their wine business. They therefore moved into the whisky trade by buying Glen Spey Distillery in 1887 in Rothes, eight years later Strathmill and in 1904 Knockando. At first Gilbey's insisted that the only Scotch whisky was malt whisky, but they had to go with the tide and enter the field of blending. 'Glen Spey' is certainly an excellent blend with a good Glenlivet flavour. They also market a twelve-year-old Irish whiskey—'Red Breast'.

During this flourishing period at the beginning of the century there emerged in the family the picturesque personality of Sir Walter Gilbey, who was well known on the turf, famous for his carriages and a friend of King Edward VII. In due course he became a baronet. Gilbey's has always been very much a family business and those who married into the family, notably the Golds and the Blyths, became active members. The headquarters and export organisation of International Distillers and Vintners is now York Gate, Regent's Park, London.

Long John International (formerly Seager Evans)

This company had its beginning in 1805 when James Seager and William Evans established themselves in Pimlico, London, as makers of 'gin and other delectable products'. At that time the world of gin flourished. The names of Gordon, Booth, Nicolson, Burnet and Tanqueray, who were contemporaries at that time, still survive. Mr Evans became a sheriff of the City of London. The firm absorbed several local distilleries including Hollands in Deptford in East London, a firm which had been established in 1779 but has now been closed.

In 1936 the executive headquarters moved to more gracious premises in 20 Queen Anne's Gate in the West End of London.

In the early part of this century the gin trade had ceased to flourish temporarily and in the 1930's the firm turned its attention to whisky by joining with Chaplins, an old-established whisky merchant in the city with old cellars at Tower Hill, London, which are still to be seen. In doing so they took over the very successful whisky 'Long John'. This whisky got its name from the owner of Ben Nevis Distillery at Fort William, long John Macdonald, who appears to have been quite a remarkable figure of great stature and physique. The whisky was of course originally a Highland malt but has been a blend since about 1909. In 1927 Seager Evans set up Strathclyde Distillery for making grain whisky, while in 1937 they took over Glenugie Distillery at Peterhead in Aberdeenshire. In 1956 Seager Evans was bought by Schenley Industries, itself now a subsidiary of Glen Alder of New York, and there began with the aid of American capital a new era of expansion. In order to be assured of still more supplies of malt whisky in 1957 they opened a new distillery, Kinclaith, near Glasgow, and at the same time greatly increased there, their facilities for storage and maturing.

The success of 'Long John' led to the building in 1958–9 of the elegant new distillery at Tormore on a tributary of the Spey a few miles north of Grantown-on-Spey. This is certainly one of the show distilleries in Scotland and such a change from the many drab places which exist, a breakaway indeed from the almost studied careless shabbiness of the Speyside distilleries. It was designed by Sir Albert Richardson, a past President of the Royal Academy. It was the first new distillery built on Speyside this century but there has been a spate of reconstruction and building since. The trade is proud of new Tormore although it is interesting to note that it makes whisky in the old traditional way. (See also Tormore.)

The company still remains a separate entity quoted on the London Stock Exchange. It has associated companies in Australia, New Zealand, Brazil and Chile, and in 1959 it acquired the well-known Coates Distillery which makes Plymouth gin, so famous in the Navy.

Laphroaig Distillery (see page 43) on the western island of Islay came into the group in 1962. The whiskies the firm now produces are 'Long John' (standard and de luxe blends), Laphroaig (a malt), 'Islay Mist' (a blend) and 'Black Bottle', through Grahams of Aberdeen.

Seagram

This company is a comparative newcomer to the world of Scotch whisky. It began in 1924 when that remarkable man Samuel Bronfman built a new distillery near Montreal in Canada, and later formed what is now the great Distillers Corporation which now has assets of £270 million. Samuel Bronfman died in 1971. In 1928 his company purchased control of Joseph Seagram & Sons which already made Canadian whiskies. In Scotland the firm began by buying one of the oldest distilleries, Milton, now known as Strathisla (see page 28) and building a new distillery of Glen Keith with Keith Maltings and Keith Bonds. Merchandising facilities were developed through the old and well-known firm of Chivas Bros. in Aberdeen (see page 29).

All this was made possible by the great success of the Canadian company. Canada is a cold place. In that country the firm's best known whisky is Seagrams, a hard dry rye whisky, while in Scotland 'Chivas Regal' stands out as a rich de luxe blend made from well-matured malts which it is said Mr Bronfman chose personally. More recently the company has marketed '100 Pipers', 'Highland Clan', 'Sheriffs', 'Sherriffs Premium' and in 1953 to celebrate the Coronation of Queen Elizabeth, 'Chivas Royal Salute', but of these I have no experience as yet.

The firm now has a striking administrative building together with a great blending and bottling plant in Paisley, while in 1971 it will have twenty-seven warehouses on a fifty-seven-acre site at Dalmuir, just north of Glasgow, where malting and blending are done. The company also sells 'White Horse' in the United States for D.C.L., from whom, in 1963, it purchased the excellent 'Burnett's White Satin gin. During the second world war Seagrams became the largest producer of alcohol in the American Continent.

Appearing over a Seagram signature is an advertisement which reads: 'We who make whisky say DRINK MODERATELY' and it goes on to say 'The real enjoyment whisky can add to the pleasure of gracious living is possible only to the man who drinks good whisky and drinks moderately. Whisky cannot take the place of milk, bread or meat. The pleasure which good whisky offers is definitely a luxury.'

Such a text must appeal to the Scottish Divine who said: 'Whisky is one of the best of God's creatures. It is only the abuse of it by man which is evil.'

Stewart of Dundee

This company is not to be confused with J. & G. Stewart of Edinburgh, although it may have had a similar origin. Who the original Stewart was appears to be obscure. It was one of the many Scottish firms founded about the middle of the last century to take advantage of the newly invented Coffey still and the benefits of blending malt and grain whiskies. It is peculiarly proud of not being part of any whisky combine and not owning any distillery, 'instead of being restricted to the economic demands inseparable from the ownership of distilleries'. It is however dependent on the goodwill and the surpluses of distilleries owned by others. By subtly combining many malts and grains Stewart succeeds in making a flavoursome and above the average blend 'Cream of the Barley', for which the demand is now so large that since 1967 they have had to increase enormously their facilities for blending and bottling in premises outside Dundee, the great jute, and now university city on the east of Scotland.

Of recent years the company has taken over Curtis, an old firm founded in the East End of London for the making of gin two hundred years ago. It later turned to the making of whisky and produced 'Scotsman's Head', which was better known abroad than at home. The current blend, in an attractive bottle, 'Curtis de Luxe', is much better, a vast improvement on the original which I knew twenty-five years ago. It is a typical modern light blend with no disagreable features, but it would benefit from more malt.

Stewart has now become the whisky division of the great and ever-growing Allied Breweries combine, which has a capital of over £92 millions and a turnover of £350 millions from its sales of beer, cider, wines and spirits. With an outlet of over 8,000 licensed houses, 1,582 shops and 52 hotels, the prospects for Stewart are rosy, quite apart from exports, but I still feel that the day is not far distant when they will reach for the dignity and prestige of owning a first class malt, even if they have, like their competitors, to build a distillery.

In the meantine through other subsidiaries such as Grant's of St James's, Harvey's of Bristol and the Victoria Wine Company, it sells many other whiskies, especially those of D.C.L.

William Teacher

William Teacher must have been a remarkable young man. He founded his firm in 1830 when he was only nineteen, and by the time he was forty he had established, under his own name, eighteen licensed retail premises. Now there are none, for the modern company, Teacher's Distillers Ltd, is concerned solely with distilling, blending and bottling. In his later years at least William Teacher was a patriarchal figure, a tall man with a flowing white beard who was a strict Victorian in the conduct of his premises and his family. Insobriety and smoking were not allowed.

The blend 'Highland Cream', on which the company now concentrates, was first registered in 1884 and the great success which it has had reflects on the skill of the founder and his successors. In 1891 Teacher built a distillery at Ardmore, Kennethmont, in Aberdeenshire, and his early blends were largely based on its products. More recently in 1962, the old distillery at Glendronach tucked away in a glen near Huntly —16 miles from Ardmore—was acquired.

Glendronach, built in 1826, was one of the earliest distilleries to be licensed and still gets power from a picturesque water wheel on the Ronach river. It produced a single malt whisky which until recently had a label with a blue tag 'most suitable for medicinal purposes'. This was removed by Teachers but serves to distinguish the earlier bottlings. It was a pleasant malt but is not a distinguished whisky.

To cope with the great demand for 'Highland Cream' the company greatly increased its facilities for blending and bottling by building in 1962 a great and very modern plant at Craig Park, Glasgow.

The business of William Teacher & Sons remained a purely family affair for three generations, but in 1923 it became a private company to enable it to deal more easily with death (estate) duty. It had a capital of £200,000, but in 1948 Teachers (Distillers) Ltd was formed first as a private company and a year later as a public company with a capital of £2 million. Now its assets are over £5 million, a remarkable achievement which speaks well for the quality of the product and the way in which its sales have been promoted all over the world in spite of the great competition of to-day. A Teacher is still chairman and the family tradition is kept up by which the board of the company solemnly sit round a table weekly and pass judgement on its product. The whisky is one of excellent quality with a pleasant sweet flavour, but slighly more peaty than 'Vat 69'.

Hiram Walker (Scotland)

Although the name of Hiram Walker is relatively new in the field of Scotch whisky, by taking over some of the oldest distilleries in Scotland the company has rapidly established itself as a major producer, blender and exporter. It received the Queen's Award for Exports in 1968.

In 1930, Hiram Walker-Gooderham & Worts of Ontario, hitherto a purely Canadian company in the liquor business, ventured to Scotland by acquiring a 60 per cent interest in the Stirling Bonding Company and that of J. & G. Stodart, who owned Glenburgie-Glenlivet Distillery a few miles west of Elgin. In 1936 they obtained the remainder of the shares and at the same time the old-established firm of George Ballantine & Sons of Dumbarton. At the same time it purchased the distillery of Milton Duff Glenlivet, which belonged to the Yool family. It is of interest that the two distilleries use the name Glenlivet although they are more than 20 miles away from the Livet.

These two distilleries are on the great barley-growing plain between Elgin and Forres. The barley now used, however, is supplied by Robert Kilgour & Co., an associated company in Kirkcaldy in Fife.

At Dumbarton, where the headquarters of Hiram Walker are, there is the Lowland malt distillery of Inverleven, but now has been added an enormous grain distillery. In addition there are maturing warehouses and a blending and bottling plant all on the same site which has a unique guard of geese, reminiscent of the geese of Capitol Hill in ancient Rome which gave the alarm of marauding Goths.

In 1955 Pulteney Distillery (see page 31) in Wick, Caithness-shire, the most northerly distillery on the mainland of Scotland, was acquired. This distillery and its excellent malt whisky, 'Old Pulteney', has already been described. In 1970 Balblair was purchased.

In 1954 Hiram Walker took over Glencadam Distillery in the old cathedral city of Brechin at the edge of the great plain of Strathmore just south of the eastern end of the Grampians in Forfarshire, and in 1954 Scapa Distillery on the island of Orkney, overlooking the famous Scapa Flow where the German fleet scuttled itself after the first world war. This distillery had been built in 1885 by a Mr J. T. Townsend, who was a well-known figure on Speyside. Now with six malt distilleries and warehouses for storing malts the group is well placed to make its very many blends.

The company does not market any whiskies under its own name. The chief product of the Hiram Walker group is the well-known and popular blend 'Ballantines', but it also markets 'Old Smuggler', 'Rare Old Highland' and the de luxe blend 'Ambassador' through its member companies.

Other companies which do not own distilleries now in the group blend 'Royal Northern Cream' (Lauder & Co.), 'Barclay's Liqueur' (Barclay & Co.), 'Argosy Scotch' (Mackenzie & Co.), 'Old Abbey' and 'The Mackintosh' (Mackintosh & Mackintosh), 'Gold Label' (Marchant), 'Old Original' (Scotia Distillers), 'Kings Choice', 'Harvest Home', 'White Broom', 'Dorus Mor' (Stewart Pott), 'Ancient', 'Antique', 'Scottish Arms' and 'Thornes Heritage' (Thorne & Sons) and 'Jamie O'Six' (Stevenson, Taylor & Co.). Indeed an impressive list. How different or how good they are perhaps I shall find out in time! Hiram Walker has followed the general pattern of D.C.L. in that it consists of a number of relatively independent companies.

William Whiteley

William Whiteley of Leith, who made the business which bears his name, was born in 1856 and died in 1941, by which time he had become the grand doyen of the Leith blenders. It was, however, his grandfather who began the business about the middle of the nineteenth century. He spent his whole lifetime in the business, and in 1922 founded the Glenforres Distillery Company, which has eighteen subsidiaries including, curiously enough, William Whiteley. The controlling company makes no fewer than a hundred brands of whisky, of which 'House of Lords' and 'King's Ransom', in squat square bottles, are the chief. The latter is issued at 82·5° proof and is correspondingly expensive. The company claims to have been the first to send its whisky round the world to improve the 'marrying' of its blends, indeed this is stamped on its bottles.

William Whiteley is specially worthy of notice because it owns what is in many ways Scotland's most picturesque distillery, Eradour, at Balnauld near Pitlochry. This gem of a distillery was built in 1827 on the side of a Highland burn with steep banks; on the other side are the houses where the workers live. It is so small that its spirit still only holds 480 gallons and the whole place can be run by three men.

Whyte & Mackay

Although this firm has only come into the picture of comparatively recent years, it was first established in 1882 when James Whyte and Charles Mackay went into partnership. At the same time they incorporated the old and still active bonding business of Allan & Paynter, which appears in the Glasgow directory of 1844, and they introduced too their 'Special'. Since its formation the growth of the firm has been steady. This has been largely the result of very original advertising and the very active promotion of a good whisky. The introduction of a measure cap to the bottle and attractive packing are examples of this. In 1960 Whyte & Mackay amalgamated with McKenzie Brothers of Dalmore, whose excellent Highland malt has already been described, to form a public holding company quoted on the Scottish Stock Exchange. Two sons of the original James Whyte are directors. A further development occurred in 1963 when the share capital was acquired of Jarvis, Halliday & Co., who were wine shippers with a world-wide sales organisation of great value in selling the whisky.

Whyte & Mackay's 'Special' is a whisky with a very light flavour to suit modern taste, 'the lightest and brightest thing about'. It contains thirty malts subtly blended, but for those who prefer a heavier blend 'Supreme', with a higher proportion of malt, is marketed, and an older variety is available '21 Years Old' for the connoisseur.

Such a bright and energetic company deserves to prosper.

William Grant

The story of this company which blends Grant's 'Standfast', has already been described on page 26.

In concluding this section on the blenders, I must regret again that it has not been possible to include many blenders who I know produce excellent whiskies. Some of these are blenders to the trade, such as Robertson & Baxter, Glasgow, and Macdonald Greenlees of Edinburgh. Such blenders make up whiskies for wine and spirit merchants and stores who want to have a blend of their own. The blenders remain anonymous. D.C.L. will also make up special blends 'if the order is large enough'!

The Royal Warrant

Only three distilleries have been authorised to use the Royal affix; Royal Brackla, Royal Lochnagar and Royal Glenury, and all in the last century.

Many blenders and wine merchants, however, have been granted the Royal Warrant of Appointment as suppliers to the Royal household and are authorised to use the Royal Arms. They are: Berry Bros. & Rudd, James Buchanan & Co. Ltd, John Dewar & Sons Ltd, John Haig & Co. Ltd, Hill Thompson & Co. Ltd, Justerini & Brooks Ltd, William Sanderson & Son Ltd, J. & G. Stewart Ltd, John Walker & Sons Ltd, White Horse Distillers Ltd, Chalié, Richards & Co. Ltd, John Begg Ltd.

They are all recognised as companies marketing whiskies of quality, and this speaks well for the popularity of blends in high places.

Buchanan, Dewar, Sandersons, John Walker and Hiram Walker, Berry Bros. and International Vinters and Distillers have received the Queen's Award for Exports.

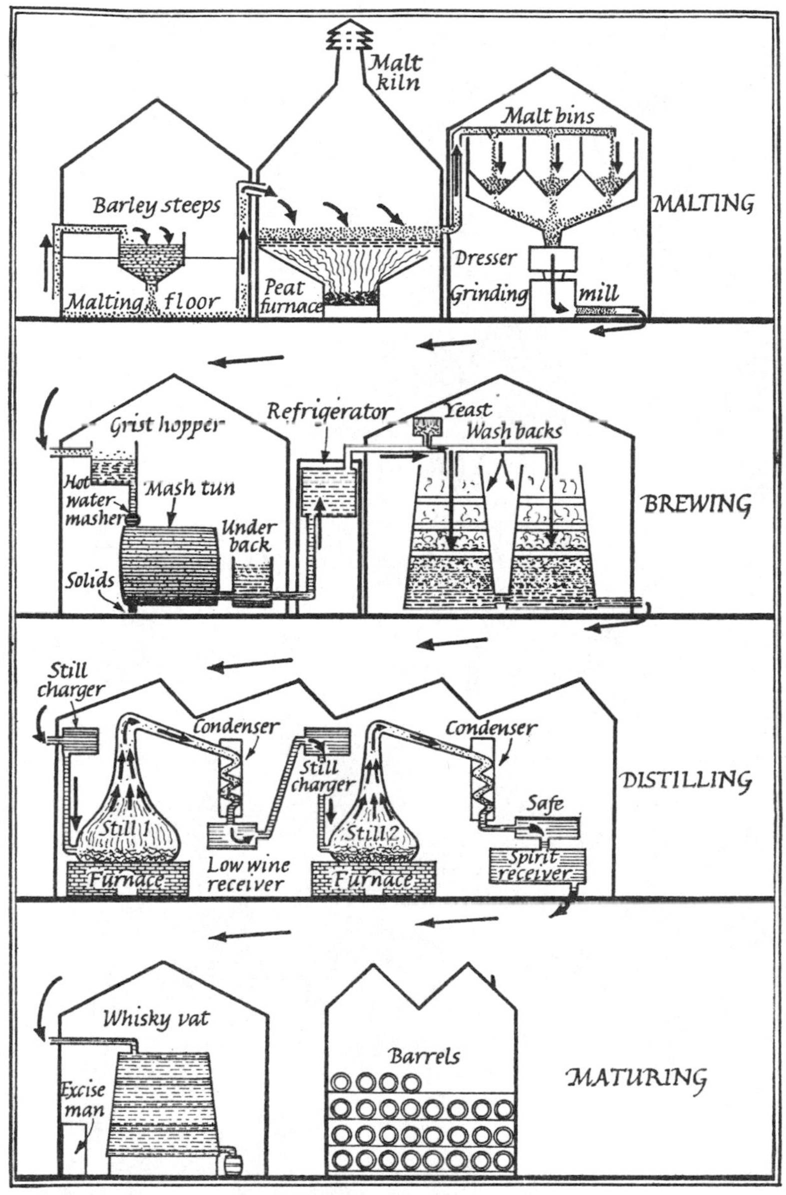

Diagram of a distillery. In many distilleries malt is purchased from maltsters heated to the degree required.

IV. The Making of Whisky

Malt Whisky

This whisky is made by malting barley, fermenting an extract of the malt with yeast, and driving off the flavoured alcohol by heat. The general method is the same in all distilleries.

Malting is done by causing the barley seeds to germinate by moistening them and keeping them at an appropriate temperature.

First the barley is steeped in water for 50–70 hours, then, by the traditional method, spread out at first two feet deep on a large concrete floor in the malting house. This is commonly a large badly lit building with a low ceiling. To prevent it from generating too much heat it is turned every eight hours, by men using wooden shovels, to reduce the damage to the seeds. This also aerates. This whole process is very laborious and takes up such a large amount of space that other methods have been introduced.

In several distilleries Saladin boxes are used. These are long concrete or metal containers in which the barley may be spread after being steeped. Thereafter the aeration is carried out by slowly revolving metal forks which gradually travel up and down the boxes. The forks make it possible for the air to reach the seeds. The method was invented by M. Saladin, a French engineer, and introduced into several distilleries in the early 1950's, the first being Glen Mhor, Tamdhu and Muir of Ord.

In other distilleries malting is carried out in enormous drums which revolve slowly, air being admitted through a central inlet. This method takes up a minimum of space. The method is used at Glen Grant and at the great malting establishments of D.C.L. at Burghead and at Ord.

In some malting establishments all three methods are in use.

The process of germination is only allowed to continue until good signs of life appear in the seed, that is, rootlets and stem have just developed. The seeds remain on the floor for 6–10 days depending on local temperature and humidity. This gives time for the maximum diastase and a small amount of maltose to be developed. If germination proceeded further the young plant would use up its maltose, as it does normally when in the soil before the root and leaves have begun to take up nourishment. Germination is slowed by allowing the seeds to dry and wither by spreading them more thinly. The 'green malt' is now ready for the kiln.

Drying and Peating. The kiln is the characteristic building of all old distilleries—with a pagoda-like ventilator at the top. Half-way up it has a perforated floor on which the germinated barley is spread and below it has a furnace. This used to be heated with peat only, but now coke is commonly used, the peat being used only to give flavour to the malt. The whole process of malting takes 9–15 days, but the period may be reduced by the use of 'hasteners' which accelerate germination. At the Moray Firth Maltings at Inverness the drying and peating is done by blowing hot peat reek into the Saladin boxes.

When dry the malt is crisp and friable like toast, pleasant to the taste and may be kept in malt bins for several weeks till required.

An increasing number of distilleries have found it more economical not to do their own malting but to buy it from maltsters ready for use and peated to whatever degree is required. Some whiskies have a more peaty flavour than others.

Many of the newer or reconditioned distilleries have no typical kiln house, or, if they have, they use it for other purposes. The larger companies have their own separate malting establishments.

Peat is decayed vegetation obtained commonly from marshy peat mosses, but not necessarily so. That from Orkney which used to be extensively exported to Scotland is obtained from hills.

Peat was, until modern transport made coal more easily available, extensively used as fuel and still is in remote country areas. It is not generally realised that peat is a very variable commodity according to the vegetation of which it is formed and to its depth. It may be three to ten feet deep and is commonly cut by hand. At its best it is, when dried, hard like coal and dark in colour, but it may be very soft and friable.

The peat reek or smoke which it emits when burned gives the pleasant characteristic aroma of burning vegetation. Nowadays a large amount of the peat used comes from Pitsligo and has a particularly penetrating aroma. A few distilleries still use local peat, indeed a local supply of peat, water and barley largely determined the location of a distillery. The peat used by Hutcheson, the maltsters of Kirkcaldy, who supply many distilleries, comes from Lanark. There is no doubt that peat is a very important factor in the flavour of whisky, but it is also used to hide the lack of flavour of a poor whisky.

Mashing and Brewing. When the malt is required it is first passed through a dresser to remove rootlets and the like. It is coarsely ground in a mill and passes in weighed amounts to a mashing machine, where it is mixed with hot water to a consistency of coarse porridge in the *mash tun*. The latter is a huge round vat, usually of cast iron, with a capacity of 2,000 to 8,000 gallons. A mash tun with a capacity of 5,000 gallons will take about 4,750 gallons of water and 400 bushels of malt (Birnie).

In the mash tun the malting action of the diastase (which is not killed by the drying) begins again and converts the remaining starch to maltose and other fermentable sugars.

After about an hour when the water has extracted most of the maltose from the seed, the *wort*, as it is now called, is drained out of the tun through its perforated bottom and conveyed to a worts receiver. The mash tun is again filled with hotter water, stirred, and again the fluid is drained off to the worts receiver or underback.

A third, but smaller amount of hot water is put into the mash tun, but this is subsequently pumped to a container to be added to the next supply of malt. The several washings ensure that none of the maltose is wasted. The residue left in the mash tun, known as the draff or grains, is removed and sold to farmers as animal food. It consists of the barley less its starch and contains protein, fat and cellulose.

Fermenting. The wort is now cooled and conveyed by pump or gravity from the worts receiver to the fermenting vats or *wash backs*. Here yeast is added to bring about fermentation. The enzymes of the yeast break down the maltose to alcohol and the gas carbon dioxide. Actually the yeast grows on the wort and these substances are by-products.

Fermentation is a very active process and may be so violent that the wash back vibrates. Undue frothing caused by gas production is controlled by stirring the surface. In some distilleries the wash back has a metal lid so that the carbon dioxide can be collected, but in most it goes to waste in the air while the alcohol remains in solution in what is now known as *the wash*. This alcohol is not, however, allowed to go much above 5 per cent concentration as it would interfere with, and eventually at 14 per cent kill the yeast. Fermentation usually ceases in 36–40 hours and the wash passes to a wash receiver. This is a large container which may receive wash from several wash backs. Here it is securely locked by the excise officer.

So far the process of whisky making is very like brewing beer. Indeed, the man in charge is known as the brewer of the distillery.

Distillation. This is the process characteristic of whisky making, indeed of all spirit making. In distillation the alcohol is separated from the wash by heating it. The alcohol is more volatile than steam and comes off first. The distilling of malt whisky is done in two stages. The first stage produces an impure dilute alcohol. This is then distilled a second time and thus the alcohol is concentrated. The distillation is carried out in a *pot still*. This is usually a large onion-shaped vessel with a long narrow neck which leads to a condensing coil or worm. Heat is applied in a variety of ways, and differs from one distillery to another. A coal fire below the still fed by mechanical stokers is one of the most common. Many modern distilleries have great central oil-fired steam boilers to provide steam which heats coils or 'kettles' in the still. The stills may or may not

The interior of a modern distillery. Commonly the condensers are on the outside of the building. (Drawn from a photograph of Glenglassaugh Distillery by kind permission of Highland Distilleries Ltd)

have insulating jackets over their lower half to conserve heat. Steam heating has the advantage that there can be no scorching of the material at the bottom of the still and a rummager is not needed. This is a chain-like contrivance which stirs the wash, and as in cooking prevents its sticking to the bottom when the fire is applied directly beneath the still.

Some insist that the direct firing of the still by extra cooking of the fluid at the bottom improves the flavour of the subsequent whisky, but nevertheless steam heating is on the increase. The still is slowly brought to the boil, so the wash is in a sense stewed before the alcohol and water vapour come off. These pass through the narrow neck of the still, usually to copper coils around which cold water flows. Here the vapour condenses into fluid now known as *low wines*. These pass through the spirit safe to the low wines receiver. Every 2,500 gallons of wash will produce from 500 to 600 proof gallons of low wines which are now redistilled.

The fluid which remains in the still, the *burnt ale*, is discarded and the still thoroughly cleaned before the next charge.

The Spirit Safe. The testing of the distillate from the stills is carried out in 'the safe'. This is an ingenious contrivance consisting essentially of a glass box, usually set in brass (some modern ones have stainless steel) through which the fluids pass in such a way that they can be tested. By turning appropriate taps, the distillate can be turned into the bottom of a cylindrical vessel in which a hydrometer is floated. From this the stillman by taking the specific gravity controls the operation of his still. He can also drip distilled water into it to see if it remains cloudless when so diluted. All this he does without handling his product let alone being able to taste it, for the spirit safe is locked by the excise officer. The original spirit safe is still to be seen in the entrance hall of Laphroaig Distillery on the island of Islay. It is surprising that those used to-day are very little different.

The second distillation is carried out in the spirit still, which is similar to, but usually smaller than, the wash still as smaller volumes are dealt with. This time very great care has to be taken to retain only that part of the distillate which has the appropriate alcohol concentration and character for what is now the new whisky. The first part of the distillate, the *foreshots*, which are too strong and impure, and the last part, the *feints*, are discarded by turning them into a feints receiver for redistillation in the next batch. No alcohol is wasted. There is no hard-and-fast line between the foreshots, the potable whisky and the feints, indeed some of the foreshots contribute to the flavour of the whisky. They contain aldehydes, furfurols and a variety of other congenerics, but too much of these would make the whisky bitter and it would be liable to become cloudy when diluted. It is in this discrimination that the stillman shows his skill. On his loving care depends the quality of the whisky.

The residue, *spent lees*, left in the second still after the distillation, is now little more than water and is run to waste. The second distillation of about 2,000 gallons of low wines takes about ten hours. Thus the process from the crushing of the malt to the production of the whisky takes about five days, while a day is needed for cleaning the stills. Sunday is commonly a day of rest, but some modern distilleries work a seven-day week.

Maturing. That whisky became better when matured in the cask was probably learnt from the brandy distillers in France, but it was quite early appreciated by the Scottish blenders. The importance of it was early recognised and written up by William Sanderson in relation to his 'Vat 69' (see page 70). In maturing whisky loses its fire, becomes less toxic and becomes tastier and smoother, but exactly what happens chemically is not known and the process cannot be hastened. By a law first introduced in 1915, primarily to reduce consumption in wartime, whisky must be kept in the cask for three years before it is sold, but the best makers of malt and grain whisky deplore its being sold before it is five years old and admit that the malt whisky is not fully matured to its best for fifteen years. This, alas, involves a large amount of capital lying idle for this period.

In maturing whisky loses a small amount of alcohol and

water according to the climate of the warehouse in which it is stored. In a wet season the whisky loses strength, but in a dry season it loses bulk. A loss of 3 per cent per year, known as 'ullage', is allowed by the revenue authorities, but more must be explained.

By tradition whisky was matured in sherry casks, probably because originally they were the cheapest casks the Scots could find. Now, when such casks are scarce for the firms who have not ancient contacts, they are a thing of the past. At least one large firm reassembles casks from America which have been used for bourbon whisky. There is, however, no doubt that sherry casks are best and do contribute a subtle something to the whisky.

Casks. Sherry casks are made from oak because of its durability, combined with the fact that they are not completely impervious.

Alcohol and water escape very, very slowly. The wood is said to be the white oak of North America, but of recent years I am assured that Spanish oak is considered adequate. A buyer commonly supplies his own casks to be filled and stored at the distillery.

Private persons can also purchase filled casks which the distillery will store at a rent, but the variability of malt whisky makes this rather a gamble.

A Highland malt is, as has been said, at its best at about fifteen years. After twenty it is liable to acquire a woodiness probably due to slight rotting of the cask. It continues, however, to improve in the bottle. It is said to 'brandify' by those who know, but for some reason, which I do not understand, the idea that a change takes place in the bottle is not generally approved of. I have three standard malt whiskies which I have had in the bottle for thirty-five years and they are better than I can buy at the moment of the same brand. It may simply be that the pre-war whiskies were better than the moderns. What little remains of them can only be described as nectar, and this opens up the whole problem of whether or not bottled whisky should not be 'laid down'.

Grain Whisky (see also page 49.)

The Patent Still. The idea that the alcohol in fermented wash could be driven off by steam was first developed by Robert Stein, a distiller in Kilbagie in Clackmanan, who patented a still on this principle in 1826. In 1830 a greatly improved version of this still was invented by Aeneas Coffey, an inspector-general of excise in Dublin, and so apparent were its advantages that its popularity grew rapidly.

In principle the still consists of two huge columns in sequence over 40 feet high, one known as the analyser and the other the rectifier. The cold fermented wort i.e. the wash, goes in at one end and trickles over a series of perforated trays, through which steam is driven from below. The steam drives off the alcohol while the cold entering wash, cools the alcohol which is condensed by a cold water coil at the top of the second or rectifying column. (See figure.)

The great advantage of the Coffey still is that it can work continuously so long as wort and steam are available, and requires much less labour than the traditional pot still. Nor does it need the same subtle skill and care of the pot stillman. The making of the alcohol is simply a chemical industrial process involving, of course, considerable accuracy. The whole process is like that of a pot distillation under the control of resident excisemen, and the output is controlled through the operation of the usual spirit safe. The alcohol which it produces is remarkably pure, as the wash is not stewed as in the pot still. There is, however, an ingenious arrangement by which the first and last parts of the distillate are redistilled.

The still is particularly suitable for producing whisky cheaply from grain or maize. When grain whisky for blending whisky is being made the maize is first ground and the starch gelatinised by steam. Then about 15 per cent of barley malt is added to the mash tun to provide the diastase necessary to break down the starch of the maize into maltose. Canadian barley which is specially rich in diastase, is commonly used for this purpose. The original Coffey still was made of wood but now it is made of

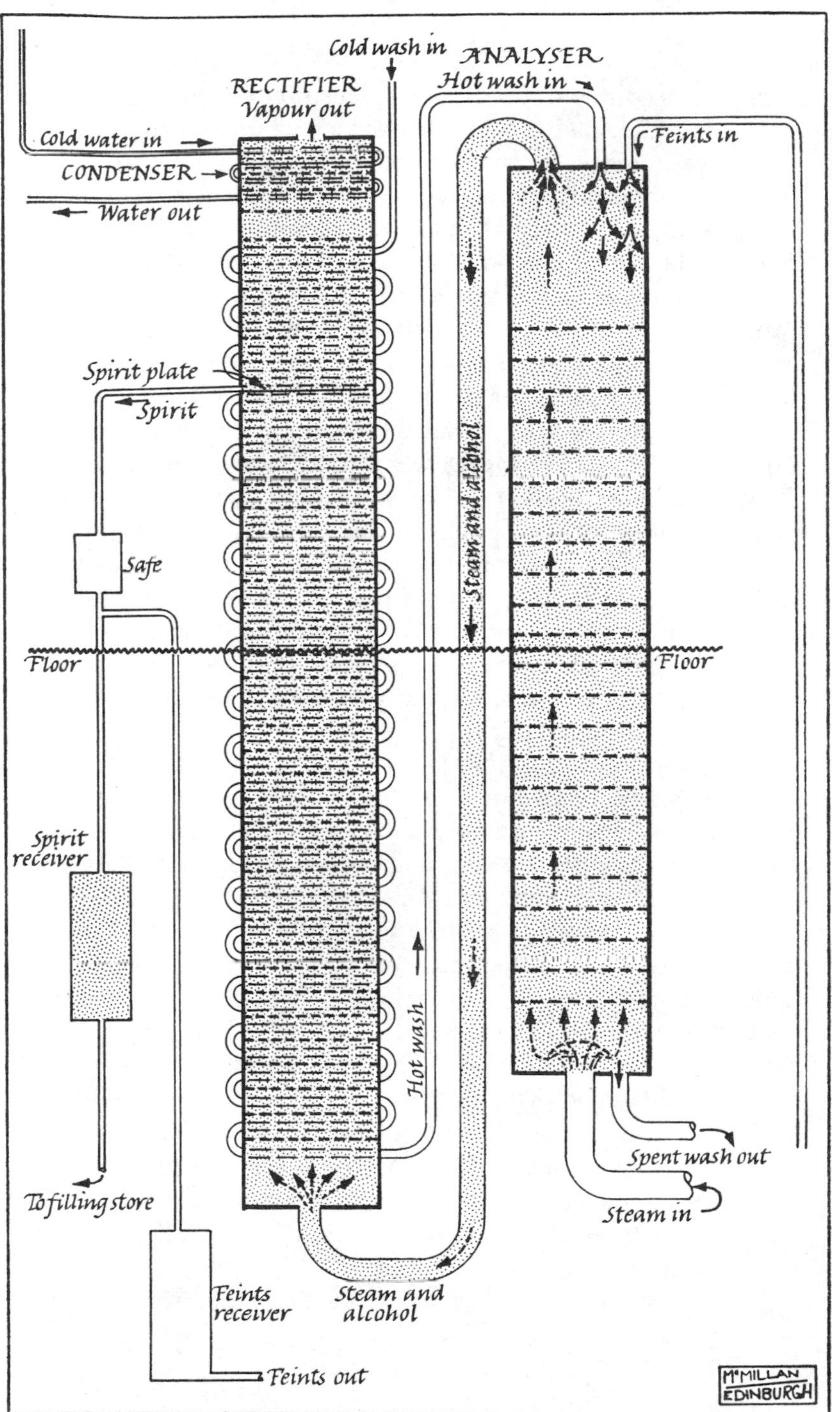

The Coffey Still

metal. Indeed this still is being replaced by a further improved version for the making of industrial alcohol and alcohol for gin.

The early history of the patent still is of some interest. When it was introduced it was taken up especially by the enterprising Stein family, who were already well established as exporters of Scotch whisky to England, and were friendly with the family of Haig. Indeed, Robert Stein's sister married a John Haig. The latter, however, died at the early age of fifty-three, leaving five sons to be educated. They went to their Uncle Robert as apprentices and thus began the great House of Haig, for four of the boys in due course ran distilleries of their own, and at one time all the surviving Lowland distilleries belonged to the Stein and Haig families. They were therefore well placed to take advantage of the benefit of the patent still. By supplying grain whisky to what were to become the blending houses the patent still was largely responsible for the beginnings of the great Distillers Company and for blending in its modern sense.

Distilleries of this type grew apace in numbers, but many did not survive the great whisky slump at the end of the nineteenth century and disappeared.

The demand for blended whisky has of recent years become so great that a new crop of giant grain stills of this type have been built. They are to be seen at Girvan in southern Ayrshire, Airdrie in Lanarkshire and Invergordon in Cromarty. The building of the latter at a place so remote and necessitating so much transport is somewhat unexpected. It was built to provide employment for Invergordon. Here men had become redundant when the naval base, which played such an important part in the activities of the North Sea Fleet during the last war, was disbanded. The buildings, which cost over £2 million, look like those of a factory rather than of a distillery, but there is an infectious enthusiasm about the place, which is run by men who, unlike those in malt distilleries, have had for the most part little to do with the making of whisky. Such enterprise deserves to flourish.

The distillery can turn out 10 million gallons of grain whisky per year and has certainly saved the town at a critical time. More recently a section for making malt whisky has been added. In addition the company also owns the Ben Wyvis Distillery, and has further increased its supply of malt whisky by building a new malt distillery at Tamnavoulin near Glenlivet. This group of concrete buildings looks very out of place in a highland scene but the cause is good.

As has been said (page 49) matured grain whisky is quite a drinkable fluid but it has not the rich flavour of a malt whisky.

The Colour of Whisky

Whisky as it comes from the still is colourless or may have a very faint straw colour. The usual colour of a whisky used to be acquired by storage in sherry casks, but since gin and whisky replaced sherry as an aperitif before dinner sherry casks have been more difficult to obtain. Forty years ago most whisky was appreciably darker than nowadays, and when the Government ordered that bottled whisky should be reduced in strength to 70° proof to conserve barley it became paler. It is said that the London clubs complained because it looked as if the whisky had been diluted by barmen, so caramel began to be added and this has continued ever since, although whisky over 70° can now be sold. The casks, however, are now said to be 'wine treated', which in practice commonly means that a cupful of cheap sherry with caramel is added to each cask. Actually some companies appear to have been experimenting with colouring matter which is less sweet and sometimes the colouring matter falls to the bottom. The clear supernatant fluid, however, tastes quite normal. I imagine the nature of this colouring is secret.

Since the demand for whisky has become so great many sherry casks are used several times and even new casks. Here it may be mentioned that casks have now become very expensive. Advantage has been taken of this by enterprising firms to extol the virtues of pale whisky, which is simply whisky which has not been artificially coloured. It becomes rather a curiosity of sufficient value to make it worth while to put on the market a small quantity of such malts as 'Smith's Glenlivet' and 'Glen Grant', which are colourless.

A whisky which has been matured in a sherry cask for fifteen years has a somewhat subtle colour which it seems to me is different from that from a wine-treated cask and may also have a faint flavour of sherry which cannot be produced by adding a little sherry to whisky.

I know of one distillery where a small pile of sherry casks with their Spanish origin marked on the end are very conspicuous at the entrance to the distillery and they do not ever seem to be changed!

The Variation in Malt Whiskies

As we have seen, the malt whiskies vary very much in character. Whiskies made in neighbouring distilleries vary like wines from adjoining vineyards and still more from different parts of the country.

No one is prepared to say why exactly this is. Much has been made of the claim that the water is a primary consideration. Some claim that the best whisky is made from water from peaty sources which trickles over granite, but granite is a very insoluble substance and certainly the water does not stay long enough on it for this to be of any importance; indeed, some of the most famous Glenlivets are made from water drawn from local wells.

One thing is certain, the major distilleries are situated in areas where there is a large rainfall and large quantities of water are needed for cooling and for extracting the malt. Soft water is as near as possible to rain water, that is almost distilled water and is certainly a much better solvent than hard water. This is well seen in relation to tea. Tea made from the hard water of London is much better than the same tea made with soft water, which is known to extract the bitter oxalic acid from it. This may produce irritation of the urinary tract in some persons, especially if they are not accustomed to it (Bell and McDowall, *Lancet*, 1940).

At one time the town council of Kirkcaldy concluded that tea was indeed more harmful than whisky!

Some soft waters are known to be lead solvent and special measures have to be taken to combat this. This special solvency power is thought to be partly due to carbon dioxide and partly to acid-producing bacteria in the peat, but the amounts present are too small to be detected. It is therefore easy to understand how soft and slightly peated water can dissolve substances other than maltose from the malt mash and it is well recognised that it is these substances which are largely responsible for the valuable characteristics of malt whisky. In this connection, too, the water may acquire further properties from the peated malt itself.

The source of the barley which is the essential and sole ingredient of malt whisky appears to be much less important than was hitherto supposed. At one time an attempt was made to restrict the name whisky to the product made from Scottish barley and sometimes a buyer would only buy barley from certain farms, indeed, only from certain fields from such farms. Originally whisky was distilled from barley grown in the neighbourhood of the distillery and it was bought in quite small quantities. Records at Royal Lochnagar Distillery near Balmoral show purchases of as little as two quarters. Now all this has changed. Highland barley is scarcely used at all and then only in good years. The Highland fields are said to be over-fertilised and to produce a barley with high nitrogen—rather than starch. This is denied by one maltster. Most comes from the rich farming lands round the Firth of Forth but much comes from the great plains of East Anglia which for centuries has been the granary of England. Now too, barley comes from such remote places as Australia, South Africa or even India, and this has the advantage of being very dry so that it keeps well. Most distilleries use mixtures of barley from different areas.

In conclusion it might be suggested that the modern practice of using 'fat' barley to produce the maximum amount of alcohol may reduce the flavour of modern whisky, although for many this makes it more palatable.

The peating of the malt with the smoke of burning peat in the kiln during the drying process is of major importance. The peaty flavour of some malt whiskies is specially prominent, for example, Tomatin, Glenfiddich, Dufftown, Clynelish, and Laphroaig. In others the peat can scarcely be detected although it may be subtly present. Some distillers indeed are beginning to question the necessity for peat, especially since labour costs have greatly increased its price. Where much peating is desired the peat reek (smoke) may be used over and over again by an arrangement of fans. (See also page 102.)

The strong flavour of some of the Islay whiskies and of Clynelish is probably due to the vegetation in the peat and, I suspect, old seaweed or some other such plant, for many to whom I have introduced these whiskies remark on a medicinal flavour somewhat like iodoform. Seaweed may contain iodine and might be a relic of the time when the peat mosses were under the sea. Even now many of the mosses are very near the sea. I have, however, not been able to detect iodine with simple chemical tests, but it is well known that iodine is difficult to detect even when it is certainly present—as in the thyroid gland.

I am assured that many distillers in the last few years have tended to reduce the amount of smokiness to make the whiskies taste less heavy.

Peat will, I feel sure, continue to be used. It would take a particularly good whisky to do entirely without it. Usually it covers a multitude of sins. (See also page 103.)

The shape of the still is claimed to affect the quality of the whisky, and certainly no distillery has dared to depart from the traditional onion shape although some have straight sides and wider necks than others, and some boil pots (bulges) at the beginning of the neck. At Glenburgie, where two pairs of stills are in use, one straight and the other rounded, it is claimed that two different whiskies are produced from the same materials in the same still-house! The excellent whisky made at Scapa is also made in 'Lomond' stills with vertical sides like a kettle.

There is, however, a very great range of size, from the minute stills of 250 gallons to the giants at Craigellachie.

Heating varies very much from distillery to distillery. For the modern stills coal or coke was until recently universal but there is no consensus of opinion on its effects, and coal, mechanically stoked, is still used in distilleries recently reconditioned by Scottish Malt Distillers.

Many of the modern stills are heated by oil or by steam generated by oil and supplied to the still by internal coil or by 'dust bin'. In the latter there is simply a large steam container. The coil is thought to be best for the first still.

The advantage of heating by steam is of course, as in the kitchen, that burning cannot occur. A rummager to keep the contents moving is not necessary and the still is easier to clean.

It must be recalled that the first stage of distillation is essentially stewing, and the time taken to reach the point when the alcohol begins to come off may be a consideration. Most readers of this book will probably not know that the flavour of porridge made from oatmeal and water flavoured with salt varies greatly according to the speed with which it is boiled. Steaming all night before it is eaten as done in Edinburgh Royal Infirmary probably makes the best porridge. Any cook will confirm that speed of cooking greatly affects the final product of many recipes.

The maturing of whisky in cask which is a major factor in the flavour of all whiskies has already been discussed on page 102.

The Mystique of Whisky Making

When all the possible causes for the variability of the flavour of different malt whiskies have been described there remains the subtle mysterious something which cannot be described even by the maker. Such things are not uncommon in other fields of life. James Braid, the great golfer, describes in his book in a chapter on long driving how one day he went out and hit a ball further than he had ever done before. How he did it he did not know but he continued to do it for many years and became Open Champion many times. I am reminded, too, of my batman Cooper in the first world war. I could throw a cricket ball one hundred yards, he could kick a football the length of a football pitch, but we could never teach each other how.

Most distillers would deny that their products vary or that there are vintages in whisky, but the more I learn about whisky, I realise that even the best malts vary from time to time. This is very difficult to explain. I have bottles of the best malts said to be of the same age which are so very different that it is difficult to believe that they are the same make of whisky. How the blenders must hate this! This makes the buying of malt whiskies to drink very difficult. You do not know exactly what you have bought until you have pulled the cork. The only way to get a standardised malt would be to put a cask of each week made into a vat and label it by the year.

The process of whisky making is somewhat like cooking. Anyone who has had experience of seeing a cooking competition can see what great variation can be produced in cakes or scones made from as near as possible identical recipes; indeed, the cooks will tell you that they cannot always tell in advance how the product will turn out. Some cooks too will tell you that they can never get pastry 'right'. So it is with whisky making; the brewer and the stillman are the cooks concerned. The brewer is concerned with the first stew in the mash tun, a process very like porridge making, the stillman is concerned with the temperature of the still and when to take off that part of the distillate which is to be whisky. Unfortunately neither, even then, can get a really good idea of his product until it has been matured. Brewers, stillmen and managers are born to the making of whisky and almost invariably in the Highlands of Scotland. They are almost a race by themselves, often poorly paid but happy and uncomplaining. They often dwell in quite remote places but they are sorry for those of us who dwell in towns for they commonly live in very pleasant places—very, very pleasant in summer. So the mystique of whisky making continues. Whether this will go on when the process becomes more and more automatic remains to be seen. The most centrally controlled plants are to be seen at Tomatin and at Caperdonich, the new distillery of Glen Grant, but there has not yet appeared, so far as I know, a plant wholly controlled by computer. It will come but by then all the good whisky will have been consumed and our successors will have nothing to compare it with, and even then the barley and the weather which affects the maturing process will vary. Even to-day we cannot tell what the whisky of fifty years ago was really like. It is to be hoped that the urge to make and sell whisky quickly and more cheaply will not lead to a deterioration of standards. Perhaps this has begun. I hate to think of it but, if it does, it will be replaced by whiskies from other countries, for there are rain and peat in both Spain and Japan.

V. Good Whisky

It has been said that there is only good and no bad whisky but some whisky is better than others.

The Benefits

The literature of our time and especially the literature of our fathers abounds with discourses on the evils of alcohol, largely a relic of the cheap gin era. To say that a large proportion of the inmates of our mental hospitals are or have been alcoholics is of course sad to contemplate, but these form part of the submerged tenth of our population who for one reason or another are unable to cope with civilisation, and would probably go under anyway.

It is more pleasant to contemplate that some of our greatest thinkers and teachers in all walks of life have partaken of and have written about the benefits of alcohol from time to time. Many of our greatest writers have been lyrical about it. David the psalmist refers to the wine which gladdeneth the heart of man. Some of us may recall the bible story when the water was turned into wine for the benefit of a wedding party (St John II. 9).

Alcohol has been taken by man for its beneficial action from time immemorial, and considering its enormous and growing consumption it is quite remarkable how little it is abused. Alcohol acts like an anaesthetic on the nervous system and is a very easily assimilated food. In the small amounts in which it is taken by intelligent persons, it acts on the higher parts of the brain and contributes beneficially to social behaviour. Experimentally it has been shown to reduce what are known as the inhibitory conditioned reflexes. These are reflexes or automatic responses which we have acquired by education by our parents, our schools and by the society in which we live. They give us self-consciousness and critical ability which in many persons are so exaggerated that they are mentally held down and retarded by their operation. Great speakers such as William Pitt took recourse to it before an important debate. Thus alcohol tends to convert a 'no' man into a 'yes' man and thus promotes mental relaxation and conviviality. Alcohol can indeed be described as an *antidote to civilisation.* As such it is much more valuable than the majority of sedatives, which Ministry of Health statistics show to be by far the commonest drugs prescribed by doctors. Unfortunately all such drugs amongst our weaker brethren can give rise to addiction as a too easy escape from civilisation. In large doses all are paralysants of the nervous system and in sufficient amounts will cause general mental deterioration and death.

It must, however, be admitted that although quite small amounts of alcohol may give Dutch courage, it cannot be shown that it increases either mental or physical performances, indeed all tests show the reverse. Moreover the individual concerned may have quite the opposite opinion. Here we have the social problem of drinking and driving with which we are all too familiar. In 1965 it was decided that a man with more than 80 milligrammes of alcohol in 100 millilitres (c.c.) of blood is culpable if in charge of a car. A rough estimate may be obtained from his expired air or urine and these may be confirmed by a blood test.

It is a common experience that alcohol is a rapid pick-me-up. It is so because it is extremely rapidly absorbed even from the stomach and, needing no digestion, it is very rapidly oxidised. As a source of energy seven grammes of alcohol, which is about the amount contained in 20 c.c. or a small whisky, yields over 70 large calories or about the same as three average slices of bread or 5 teaspoonfuls of cane sugar.

The effects of alcohol on the brain depend on its concentration in the blood and that in turn depends on three factors, the speed with which it is absorbed into the blood, the speed with which it is oxidised or burnt by the body and the speed with which it is excreted. Excretion takes place by the lungs, the kidneys and by the skin. A given amount is more rapidly excreted if taken with a large amount of water and the excretion of water is likewise promoted by alcohol, which is a diuretic. If a litre of water is taken it is excreted much more rapidly if alcohol is added. This is very readily confirmed. Rapid excretion takes place in hot atmospheres when the skin is sweating, and a man who has taken alcohol may be quite sober in a hot atmosphere, but going outside into cold air which shuts down the skin vessels may have an adverse effect.

Absorption may be slowed down by the simultaneous taking of food, especially fatty articles of diet or milk. This action of food may not be entirely due to delay of absorption, the carbohydrate may somehow facilitate the oxidation of the alcohol. When severe exercise is or has been taken alcohol has appreciably less effect. Those who take large amounts of exercise are much more difficult to anaesthetise. I once had great difficulty in trying to anaesthetise a Highland ghillie; indeed, he could only be 'put under' with pure chloroform, quite a risky procedure. Those accustomed to alcohol can readily appreciate by their sensations that a given amount of alcohol taken a long time after the last meal has much greater effects.

Some individuals seem to acquire a considerable tolerance to alcohol. It may be that by usage such persons have more rapid powers of oxidation and excretion, but it may be in part that they have become accustomed to adapt themselves to its action. Conscious of having taken alcohol, and being familiar with the symptoms produced, they may be more careful in their actions. It is quite fantastic how much alcohol some men can take without apparent effect.

Alcohol has a considerable effect in stimulating the activities of the digestive system and is prescribed by doctors for this reason especially in the elderly. It acts as a stimulus to peristalsis but especially it causes an increased secretion of the saliva and other digestive juices. It is because of this that if taken too strong on an empty stomach it is liable to cause an excessive secretion of acid which is so disagreeable. This commonly occurs during the night when the food has passed on from the stomach and the sympathetic (that part of the nervous system which is specially concerned with activity) is least active. Strong alcohol may cause acute irritation of the stomach wall with nausea and vomiting. It is therefore to be avoided or taken dilute by those with gastric ulcers. In some it is liable to produce bleeding. It does however help to sterilise the upper part of the alimentary tract and protect against disease. 'The best excuse for a nightcap I have ever heard of.'

Alcohol is also an active dilator of the blood-vessels, which is well seen in the skin where it produces flushing. By its profound dilator effect it causes pooling of the blood in the blood-vessels and so reduces the venous pressure, thus giving the heart less work to do (McDowall, 1925). This no doubt explains the temporary benefit from taking alcohol experienced by patients with congestive failure of the heart. There is some evidence too, that coronary thrombosis is more common in abstainers.

The great dilatation of the blood-vessels of the skin causes a sensation of warmth like a hot bath, but it causes the body to lose heat and may produce a slight fall of body temperature. It is therefore not so good to take whisky to 'keep out' the cold as is popularly supposed.

There is also the other side of the picture as Gilbert and Sullivan sang it:

A taste for drink combined with gout
Had doubled him up for ever,
Of that there is no manner of doubt,
No probable, possible, shadow of doubt,
No possible doubt whatever.

Classically, alcohol is stated to promote sexual desire, but according to Shakespeare it reduces the performance, again possibly because of the lowering of the venous pressure.

In conclusion it may be said that in spite of its disadvantages and its abuse by the few, alcohol has made the world a happier place and by promoting mental relaxation has increased the span of life. Raymond Pearl, the American statistican, has found that although heavy drinkers tend to die early, moderate drinkers have a greater expectation of life than teetotalers. This indeed is common experience.

God in his goodness gave the grape
To feed both great and small
'Tis little fools who drink too much
And big fools not at all.

The Characteristics

A good whisky should have a pleasant subtle aroma of peat, flowers and alcohol (some say of old-fashioned peardrops), which comes off especially in a warmed glass. In this it resembles a good red wine or brandy. The addition of ice or even soda water of course reduces the flavour but at the same time reduces any harshness a poor whisky may have. Whisky should be taken with water—preferably soft water—but I have made the experiment that there is not so much in this as is popularly supposed. When drunk, a good whisky is smooth and is not harsh to the throat when diluted with its own volume of water. It can be held in the mouth without producing an undue sense of burning, but it must be understood that a 100° proof or even 85° will taste stronger than one of 70° proof. The stronger the whisky the more easily the aroma comes off because of the volatility of alcohol. Some whiskies are sweeter than others, especially those to which much caramel has been added to darken the colour. A good whisky should never taste bitter but some whiskies taste medicinal.

A good whisky in moderate amounts should produce no delayed effects such as headache or sickness. The latter is commonly due to gastritis, the result of drinking too strong whisky on an empty stomach, but a so-called 'hangover' can be produced by a malt whisky under five years old and is due to the impurities which disappear during maturation in an oak cask.

The Choice

When there are so many good whiskies about, the choice of a whisky may be a problem. For most people the choice is determined by the price and by what is available and this in turn is determined by the activities of enterprising salesmen and the profit which can be made. There may be other considerations at which we can only guess. At the same time we must realise that a wine merchant or a bar cannot be expected to stock all the forty odd malts at all the different ages or the two thousand or so blends which are available. Usually we can get a few of what are known as the standard blends sold at a standard price, but a few shops and bars pride themselves on their selection.

Alas how often we hear 'Scotch and soda please'. If the whisky is needed as a pick-me-up after a tiring day it is enough to get any of the well-known blends. It is surprising, however, how many don't seem to care what whisky they drink, and few are prepared to pay more for the better blends or malts. They may even say 'they are all the same to me'. That of course is true of many of the blends. 'Don't give me your best whisky,' I am often told, 'it would just be wasted.' Poor souls, they are like those who scarcely know when the band is playing 'God Save the Queen' or 'The Blue Danube'.

People often ask what is the best whisky and I reply by asking what is the best sweet (candy in America). Is it chocolate, peppermint or toffee? Of course it all depends on your taste and extravagance, at the time.

Finally it must be said that the taste of any whisky depends on the circumstances in which it is taken. Before a meal or if you are thirsty after golf any good dry blend, like a dry sherry, tastes good, but the same whisky after a sweet will, like a dry wine, taste dreadful. Then a rich Glenlivet is desirable. It is so easy to make the experiment. On the other hand after a rich whisky most blends taste thin, therefore if you don't want to be too extravagant begin with a blend, never with a malt. Most blends can be greatly improved by the addition of a small quantity of a good malt, again an easy and economical experiment!

If your guest is one who wants ice, soda, fruit juice or still worse, ginger, then give him the cheapest whisky you have, indeed, it is best to keep some of this, the cheapest stuff, handy for there are many such. Such additions completely hide the taste of whisky as they do of wine. Americans generally have poor tastes in such matters. They prefer all drinks cold, forgetful of the fact that the bouquet of whisky or wine does not come off cold fluids. Whisky 'on the rocks', that is on ice, whisky 'sour', i.e. with lemon and sugar, or whisky 'old fashioned', i.e. with angostura, soda and fruit, are therefore most popular. This may be a relic of the time when good whisky was very scarce or of the cocktail period.

A word about chlorinated water is perhaps not out of place as it is so common nowadays. The chlorine imparts a disagreeable flavour to whisky as it does to tea, but this can be got rid of completely by boiling the water vigorously for five minutes or by aerating it by pouring it several times before use.

In these days when whisky is so popular as an aperitif, it should be noted that highly flavoured biscuits and the like spoil the taste of good whisky, especially onion, cheese and salt. Experiment has shown that liver or kidney pâté on an unflavoured biscuit is best. It is well to note too that to bring out the flavour of a whisky an equal amount of water is usually necessary, but the optimum depends on the individual whisky and on its strength. Peaty whiskies taste better diluted, a most economical experiment.

> So let us with old Omar Khayyam drink
> And drive our sorrows where we cannot think
> At least a while.

VI. Whisky Control

The Exciseman

Every distillery has at least one exciseman, more politely called the excise officer. He is the watch-dog of the Government and it is his job to see that all alcohol made is recorded in order that duty may be paid. To facilitate this, stills with a capacity of under 400 gallons are illegal unless special permission is granted (1952). Several excisemen are under the supervision of a surveyor.

Control begins as soon as the worts go into fermenting vats—the wash backs. From the volume of the contents and its sugar content the amount of whisky which is to be produced can be estimated. After the alcohol is made all the receivers and other containers and, as has been said, the all-important safe are locked up by the exciseman. The pipes in which the clean alcohol goes are by law coloured black, the pipes for the wash are painted red, while those for the low wines, feints and foreshots are blue. This ensures that they can readily be inspected. Every stage in the process is carefully supervised and when in due course the new whisky is put into casks, the excise officer must be present to record the amounts made during the week. If there is only one officer only one process can be carried out at a time so that adequate supervision can be exercised.

The casks are transferred to the warehouse for maturing and here again they are placed under lock and key by the distiller and the excise officer and cannot be removed without the knowledge of both. Such whisky is said to be *in bond* and duty is not paid till the whisky leaves for the bottler. In some cases for convenience, however, the latter may have a bonded warehouse to which the casks may be conveyed while still in bond. This avoids paying duty on accidental breakages and is to be preferred.

All this sounds a bit clumsy and suspicious and is for the

most part a relic of the old days when the duty was even more resented by the distillery owners than now. It is, however, really an advantage to the owners as it prevents pilfering at any stage. Even a vat of wash is a temptation to some men.

So we can see that the exciseman is a much busier person than sometimes appears if we visit a distillery, but I must confess I have been to a distillery where the warehouse was wide open and the excise officer was nowhere to be seen. When I remarked on this I was told, 'He trusts us. Maybe he's at the fishing but he keeps wonderful books.' We must remember that the Spey has wonderful fish in September when it is getting near the end of the salmon season. Some excisemen have had time to become novelists; of these Neil Gunn and Maurice Walsh are well known, while Robbie Burns had time to write many of his poems while he was an excise officer in Dumfries.

The exciseman is now a respected government servant, but as we are reminded by Robert Burns in his poem 'The Deil's awa' with the exciseman', he was long the butt of the distillers and the public. Many and varied are the tales of the devious methods by which in times past even the distillers and especially the smugglers, as the illicit whisky makers were called, tried to outwit him. As we have said, the apparatus needed to make whisky in small quantities is comparatively simple: some form of boiler by which heat could be applied to the fermented barley, a copper coil or worm immersed in cold water to act as a condenser for the alcoholic vapour, and a receiver. One of the great difficulties was the transport of the illicit whisky to centres of population. It must be recalled that in the eighteenth century the roads were few and easily guarded by the excise officers, so the precious fluid had commonly to be taken by horseback at night over the hills. The smuggling of whisky, like the smuggling of brandy and wines from the Continent, was for many reasons an exciting and dangerous pastime. Many of the exploits of the smugglers are recorded by Barnard, Bruce Lockhart and Ross Wilson, and more recently by Sillett.

After the rebellion of 1745 General Wade set out to give the

Highlands new roads and the country was opened up as never before. Later the advent of the train and the motor car made surveillance much more easy. The illicit still is almost a thing of the past, but there are not a few who think that the present taxation of the national drink is sure to lead to trouble, as it almost amounts to prohibition for so many.

Proof

The use of the word 'proof' is at first confusing. It indicates the concentration of alcohol in the whisky. A whisky is described as 70° or 80° proof and its price varies accordingly. The old terminology used to be 30° or 20° under proof, but this terminology has now been given up. The term 'proof' continues to be used, however, because it refers to the simple way by which the amount of alcohol in gin or whisky is measured.

The term 'proof' first referred to the concentration of alcohol in water which would just allow gunpowder to ignite, but in 1823 this was replaced by measurement of the specific gravity of the fluids by the Sikes hydrometer which had been invented in 1818. The principle of the hydrometer is simple.

If we cork or seal a piece of thin glass tubing at each end it will float in water and keep upright if it is weighted slightly at one end, say with a glass bead. A small portion will, however, be under the water but the amount under will be less if we add salt or sugar to the water to make its specific gravity greater.* It is for this reason that we can float more easily in salt water than in fresh. We can easily arrange, as Bartholomew Sikes did, the weight of the tube and graduate it so that it floats 50 per cent of its length in a mixture of equal parts of alcohol and water.

The more alcohol in a whisky or a solution, the lower the hydrometer reads because its specific gravity is less than that of water, that is, it is lighter than water. If a bottle of whisky has been standing for some time the bottle should be shaken before use as the alcohol rises to the top and the first drink may be stronger than the rest.

* Alcohol has a specific gravity of 0·793. Water is 1.

More accurate methods of analysis, the preparation of purer alcohol and the fact that equal amounts of fluids by volume did not give the same figure as equal amounts by weight and were affected by temperature, led to the need for a more accurate definition. This appeared in an Act as recent as 1952, Clause 127(2), and reads as follows: 'Spirits shall be deemed proof if the volume of the ethyl alcohol contained therein made up to the volume of the spirits with distilled water has a weight equal to that of twelve-thirteenths of a volume of distilled water equal to the volume of the spirit, the weight of each liquid being computed at 51° Fahrenheit.' So simple? So official!

In practice a temperature of 60° F. is found more convenient because it is a common temperature in 'the safe' (see page 106), and at this temperature proof contains 49·28° by weight or 57·1° by volume and proof is in fact still measured by a simple Sikes hydrometer. 70 per cent proof corresponds therefore to 40 per cent pure spirit and is usually written 70° proof.

A hydrometer is normally locked in the 'safe' so that it can measure the amount of alcohol in the effluent from the still and condenser as desired (see page 104). It can also be used separately to measure the gravity of the 'wash' before distillation.

Alcohol as it comes off a Coffey still (see page 111) is at about 165° proof, but whisky as it leaves a spirit pot still is at about 125° proof but becomes less as the distillation proceeds. It loses alcohol in the cask and a loss of 3 % per year is allowed by the excise. A loss of more than this requires investigation and may have to be paid for. Whisky is matured at 110°; at bottling it is usually diluted to 70°, 75° or 80°, but a few whiskies can be obtained at 100° proof or more. Till 1917 the usual brands were bottled at 75°, but when in wartime cereals became scarce they were by law reduced to 70°, and although this rule has now been rescinded, the whisky trade saw its advantages and retained the 70°. More water is sold!

If ignited in a saucer 70° whisky will scarcely burn, 80° burns freely and 100° so freely that all the water in the whisky evaporates: an amusing after-dinner experiment—but such waste!

Alcohol boils and becomes a gas at 78·3° C. or 174° F., that is considerably below the boiling point of water, but it will come off slowly from a bottle of whisky at room temperature (like the gas from soda-water but slower) if left in an uncorked bottle. More waste! A good whisky, however, never loses its bouquet although it may lose its alcohol and practically all taste. This was an unexpected and accidental observation.

The alcoholic content of various common liquors in *percentages* is:

Whisky or brandy	35–50
Port and sherries	15–20
Wines	7–10
Beer	3– 7
Cider	2– 6

Special beers are, however, made up to 13 per cent which is about the maximum which can be attained without distilling because the action of the yeast is stopped by the alcohol. Ports and sherries are fortified by the addition of spirit.

Standard brands of whisky are exported to the United States at 86·8° proof, but since the definition of proof is different there, this corresponds to 75° proof in the United Kingdom.

Taxation and Cost

The taxation of the national drink of Scotland may be fairly said to be a scandal, for by it the cost of whisky has been put beyond the purse of many native Scots and all because they have made it so good that it has become popular with the natives of England and America. Whisky its taxed more than any other commodity relative to its cost of production. At present it is £2·20 on a bottle at 70° proof.

The Dutch apparently first had the courage to tax alcohol, but the parliamentarians of England rapidly took up the idea—actually to finance the army in 1643. Scotland followed the next year and levied a duty of 37½p per English gallon of *aqua vitae*, the strength, however, not being specified. For a period the tax on Scotch whisky appears to have lapsed but it was reimposed in 1693. The Board of Excise was set up in 1707 and has levied duty ever since. It was about this time that gin began to be imported from Holland and by 1724 the gin age was on the way. Two factors contributed to its inception. Cheap gin began to be made in England partly as a compliment to William and Mary who had come from Holland, and also because the English armies of Marlborough fighting in that country had learnt to drink it. There was such a wave of crime in the country that something had to be done about it. Anti-gin Acts were passed in 1729 and 1736, but the latter especially was too severe to be effective and only led to more evil and law breaking. They had to be repealed in 1743. It is of interest that in our time a too severe tax on whisky and prohibition in America had quite the opposite effects to what were intended.

These laws against gin had, however, shown the legislators how money could be raised easily and during the period of the Pitts a series of Acts were passed which were never satisfactory because the taxes were based on the size of the apparatus rather than its output.

There was a race between the excise and the whisky distillers, who more frequently, by filling their stills, produced more than had been expected. Meantime illicit small stills flourished and produced half the total product. There were said to be 200 such stills in the small area of Glenlivet.

We have already referred (page 11) to the great improvement which occurred in 1823 when small stills could be licensed cheaply and a very small tax was placed on the output of the still in terms of alcohol. This was made possible by the introduction of the hydrometer (1818). The Act worked because it had the support of the local landlords and made it scarcely worth while to distil illicitly. In a few years the production of the Coffey still (1830), which made cheap alcohol, and the repeal of the corn laws (1846), which greatly reduced the price of imported maize for this type of still, slowly but surely put the illicit stills out of business. Better communication, too, made them more difficult to conceal. This done, successive governments have slowly increased the tax on whisky.

An outstanding jump in the tax occurred when Lloyd George increased the tax from 11*s*. to 14*s*. 9*d* (55p to 74p) per proof gallon. It produced bitter feelings everywhere. When the price of a nip of whisky went up from 4*d*. to 5*d*. (1½p to 2p) the 'friends of the market' in Kirkudbright went on strike and refused to drink, but the strike did not last more than ten days! A new era in the taxation of whisky had begun and the chairman of The Distillers Company spoke in 1909 of 'the dark cloud hanging over our trade'. How dark the cloud was to become he little knew.

The Scottish people have taken so many knocks that they have learnt to take them with equanimity. This was well shown by the wife of a part-time country stone mason, Geordie Tamson, whom I knew in my youth. When she was told of the great rise in the price of a bottle she just said, 'Weel, weel, Geordie will just have to work another day next week.'

In 1895 the tax on whisky was cut to 10*s*. 6*d*. (52½p) per proof gallon, but it was slowly raised till by 1918 it was £1·50. In the next three succeeding years it was raised each year until in 1920 it became £3·62½. The second world war saw still further increases until by 1948 it was £10·54 per gallon. In 1965 it became £24·60 or £1·70 a bottle, although this was slightly offset by a reduction of the retail price. A further increase to £2·20 occurred in 1970. Unfortunately, too, these increases have set a bad example to other countries to whom it is increasingly difficult to export.

The price of whiskies is now largely determined by taxation. At 70° proof, it is in 1971 £2·72 a bottle, that of the de luxe blends and the average malts £3. The price of the standard blends is made up as follows, but approximately:

The producer	£0·27
Duty	£2·20
Wholesaler Retailer	} £0·25
	£2·72

The producer may be the wholesaler.

Retailers who buy large quantities for each obtain large discounts which they may or may not pass on to the customers. Whisky by the case is about 20p cheaper.

When the proof is more than 70° the duty is automatically more and the price more. Malt whiskies usually cost a few shillings more than the blends, but I notice that of recent years there has been a tendency for those prices to rise disproportionately. Thus if a malt whisky at 70° proof is £3, at 80° the price is £3·50 and at 100° £4·50 or more. Only malt whiskies are issued so strong. In addition there is a further price increase for age. Thus the same 70° proof malt whisky which will cost £3 at seven years old, may cost £3·85 at fifteen years old. The best malts cost even more.

What is, however, called the standard price refers to the price per bottle charged by the average wine merchant when the price was controlled by the trade, but he now can charge what he likes. Quite a number of merchants in order to secure custom may sell at almost the wholesale price, i.e. £2·75 or even less, and rely for their profit on the quantity sold and the fact that they attract to their shops customers who may buy other things such as wines or groceries. The better the address of the shop the dearer the whisky. At the other end of the scale a fashionable bar or restaurant, may, indeed usually does, charge appreciably more than the standard price, and we also have the absurd situation of some retailers charging more than standard prices for whiskies which are actually cheaper to produce simply because they have an unusual name. They had better be nameless but they are usually recognisable by being tasteless.

Until recently difficulty arose in regard to measures used in bars. Usually they were termed 'single' or 'double', but some have a 'club' or a 'noggin' which was intermediate. A further difficulty arose in that the Scottish measures were larger than the English. The whole position has now been regularised. From 1st August 1966, spirits may be sold only in quantities of one-sixth gill, one-fifth gill or one-fourth gill or multiples of these quantities. The usual English 'single' has been one-sixth gill, which is the equivalent of almost 32 drinks out of the usual bottle of 26⅔ fluid ounces. This odd figure results from the fact that tax is levied per gallon—a case of whisky contains 12 bottles or 2 gallons. In practice the barman commonly pays his employer for 30 drinks out of each bottle and gets the remainder for himself. The actual cost paid by the customer still of course depends on where it is bought.

The penal taxation on whisky has however had advantages to the community as a whole. As a result of it the Exchequer raised, in 1969, no less than £126 million from spirit sold at home and abroad.

It is interesting to contemplate that in order to meet national commitments the income-tax would have to be raised, even for the teetotallers, very considerably. So the whisky drinkers benefit the community. This crippling duty says much for the popularity of whisky, but the State has begun to maim the goose which lays the golden eggs. Exports of whisky to all countries had a value of over £194 million. Half of this went to the U.S.A. Whisky makes therefore a major contribution to our ever-important balance of payments. (See tables on page 141.)

The Worshipful Company of Distillers

This is one of the ancient guild companies of the City of London. It was begun curiously enough by two doctors. The founder was Sir Theodore de Mayerne, who was physician to Charles I, a French protestant born in Mayerne near Geneva, but who had an M.D. of Oxford, in conjunction with a Dr Thomas Cadman, physician to the Queen. The latter became the first Master. Sir Theodore, who was a notable *bon viveur*, died it is said from drinking bad wine in a tavern in the Strand. He was commemorated by a bust and tablet in the Church of St Martin in the Fields nearby. It is alas now neglected in the chapel vestry of the crypt.

The Trade, as it is called, has five city companies, The Vintners, The Distillers, The Coopers, The Brewers and the

Inn-holders. The Vintners is the oldest. It was granted by Edward III in 1363 the exclusive privilege of trading in the wines from Gascony. The City companies have been called 'The Soul of the City of London' for they set the first standards of preparation and workmanship in many crafts, while they devote a large amount of their income to good works.

When the Company of Distillers was incorporated and granted arms in 1638 it was given extensive powers and important duties under the Crown for the regulation of the Trade of Distillers and Vinegar makers (from wine) and those engaged in the preparation of strong waters and of making Beergar (from beer) and Alegar (from ale) in the cities of London and Westminster, the suburbs and liberties and within 21 miles therefrom. The Company possesses its livery under the Court of Aldermen of 1672 and of the Court of Common Council in 1774. Its motto is paraphrased from Deuteronomy XXXII 2: 'Droppe as Raine distil as Dewe'.

In the reign of James II the limits of the Company's jurisdiction were extended to 31 miles, and it still acts under an ordinance of 1689 in the reign of William and Mary.

To-day however the Company has lost its monopolies and has no function in relation to the Trade, but like most City companies owns land and buildings. With the income from these it endows scholarships to assist young members of the Trade to increase their knowledge of whisky distilling and blending.

The Company of Distillers was until recently the only City company which restricted the persons who followed its craft, and by an oath of the reign of George IV every liveryman had to promise to conceal and keep 'all the lawful secrets of the Trade art and mystery'. Some of its past masters are well known in the Trade, Gordon and Burnett of gin fame, Sir Reginald Macdonald-Buchanan and J. A. Dewar. Lord Dewar, as he became, was master for four successive years.

An important function is also to provide occasion for social intercourse, for as the Archbishop of Canterbury said in 1930 on replying for the guests at a dinner of a City company: 'In these days of rush, haste and vulgarity it is good to dine from time to time in tranquil leisure and dignity.' This could indeed be taken as a text.

In Edinburgh distilling was placed under the supervision of the Royal College of Surgeons. At that time, 1505, the trade of distilling was said to be at a very low ebb in regard to quality and it was this no doubt which gave the doctors their interest.

The Scotch Whisky Association

In 1917, an unincorporated body known as the Whisky Association was established in London, with branch offices in Scotland and Ireland. It was governed by a council made up of elected members of the trade and its membership was open to distillers, blenders, owners of proprietary brands and exporters of Scotch and Irish whisky. In 1940 the Scottish branch became the principal office and its secretary, P. H. Hogg, later of John Haig, assumed the duties of Secretary of the Association.

May 1942 saw the dissolution of the association. Since the constitution was no longer in accordance with the method of carrying on the association's business and it carried no provision for alteration except by obtaining the written consent of every member, a Special General Meeting in Glasgow took the alternative of passing the resolution 'that the Whisky Association be dissolved'.

In 1942, the Scotch Whisky Association was formed, unincorporated, to take over the functions of the Whisky Association. In December 1953, the association moved its offices to their present location, 77 George Street, Edinburgh.

A further development came as a result of a legal action brought by the association in France during 1958. Although the court found in favour of the association on the merits of the case, the action was dismissed on the grounds that the association, being unincorporated, was not a competent party. The Council, therefore, considered the advantages and disadvantages of incorporation and after seeking legal advice, it was decided to recommend that the association be incorporated as a company limited by guarantee.

In 1960 the Scotch Whisky Association was incorporated under the Companies Act, 1948, on 22nd April (the word 'limited' being omitted by licence of the Board of Trade).

Membership of the Scotch Whisky Association, which is by election by the Council, may be applied for by individuals or companies who are distillers, blenders, owners of proprietary brands, brokers or exporters of Scotch whisky.

The aims of the association are: to protect and promote the interests of the industry at home and abroad; to originate, promote, support or oppose legislative or other measures directly or indirectly affecting the industry; to enter into legal proceedings in any part of the world in defence of the interests of the industry; to collect statistical and other information relating to the industry and to supply members with such information.

This information service provides a variety of commercial and legal advice and is freely available to members. The association can assist with the registration of United Kingdom and overseas trade marks; its Labelling panel can provide legal opinion on the suitability of members' labels for particular markets. It maintains an extensive file on export procedure and tariff information; statistics on all aspects of the industry are constantly brought up to date.

A special committee of the Council is responsible for the promotion and development of Scotch whisky sales at home and overseas. Their work is implemented by the association's office in London, which is concerned with the production and distribution of films and publications about the industry and the dissemination of general information on Scotch whisky on an international scale, through the media of the press, broadcasting, trade fairs and exhibitions.

Recently the Association has opened a smart office with a demonstration centre at 17 Half Moon Street, London W.1.

The present membership of the association is 155.

Statistics of Whisky

The Popularity of Whisky

The following tables show the great increase in the consumption of whisky in different countries in the last few years. They show how important the U.S.A. is to the market.

World Consumption of Scotch and Northern Ireland Whisky in regauge proof gallons

Country	*1959*	*1973*	*Country*	*1959*	*1973*
Argentine	99,709	740,327	Japan	188,271	6,537,952
Australia	1,077,314	2,446,076	Kenya	80,094	120,087
Bahamas	58,689	133,099	Lebanon	62,231	275,247
Belgium	314,979	1,670,777	Malaysia	106,400	73,315
Bermuda	44,572	65,427	Netherland		
Brazil	132,054	1,677,672	Antilles	100,050	418,844
Canada	1,019,758	1,700,188	Netherlands	124,788	812,172
Chile	60,608	16,818	New Zealand	402,922	635,519
Colombia	39,782	404,744	Norway	70,484	338,105
Cuba	81,644	4,013	South Africa	476,556	1,229,863
Denmark	124,958	473,124	Spain	31,988	1,397,646
Egypt	60,094	132,033	Sri Lanka	25,525	12,736
Finland	47,771	431,532	Sweden	201,293	902,709
France	281,073	3,295,515	Switzerland	111,450	651,763
Ghana	68,734	25,062	Trinidad	102,277	108,768
Gibraltar	50,434	36,594	United States	12,098,200	32,942,590
Great Britain	6,862,000	15,347,000	Uruguay	70,046	88,630
Hongkong	65,965	555,386	Venezuela	278,248	902,882
India	122,103	128,179	West Germany	420,153	2,917,911
Indonesia	16,657	56,061	Other Countries	2,725,372	9,967,026
Irish Republic	108,170	439,551			
Italy	132,967	3,683,721	Totals	28,548,383	93,796,664

by permission from The Scotch Whisky Association

Production and Sales

Production and Stocks (thousands of proof gallons)

Year ended 30th Sept.	*Production*	%	*Stocks*	%
1960	66,900	+18·0	277,850	+11·4
1961	70,220	+ 5·0	308,000	+10·9
1962	76,663	+ 9·2	340,000	+10·4
1963	87,255	+13·8	380,500	+11·9
1964	108,091	+23·9	432,800	+13·7
1965	126,455	+17·0	501,600	+15·9
1966	134,471	+ 6·3	572,500	+14·1
1967	123,971	− 7·8	633,000	+10·6
1968	113,606	− 8·4	675,700	+ 6·7
1969	125,999	+10·9	727,500	+ 7·7

Home and Export Sales (thousands of proof gallons)

Calendar Year	*Home*	%	*Export*	%	*Total*	%
1960	7,261	+5·8	23,147	+ 6·7	30,408	+ 6·5
1961	7,911	+9·0	26,825	+15·9	34,735	+14·2
1962	7,908	−0·04	30,070	+12·1	37,978	+ 9·3
1963	8,666	+9·6	31,773	+ 5·7	40,439	+ 6·5
1964	9,248	+6·7	35,019	+10·2	44,267	+ 9·5
1965	9,035	−2·3	39,667	+13·3	48,702	+10·0
1966	9,048	+0·1	41,596	+ 4·9	50,644	+ 4·0
1967	9,184	+1·5	43,146	+ 3·7	52,330	+ 3·3
1968	9,829	+7·0	59,155	+37·1	68,984	+31·8
1969	9,233	−6·1	52,427	−11·4	61,660	−10·6

These interesting figures show that there is now over ten years supply of whisky in the country and this is all to the good from the point of view of future blends, although it may not entirely please the producers.

POSTSCRIPT

The Future of Whisky

No Scot can think of the future of whisky without some apprehension. More whisky is being produced to-day than ever in its history and most of it is sold to blenders, some of whom are more concerned with making money now than for the future. The greatly increased production in the last few years has been primarily of the cheaper grain whisky made from maize, but this in turn has increased the demand for malt whiskies to give it flavour. Many malt distillers sell it at the legal minimum three years, and long before it is properly matured, because they have not space enough to store it. Moreover the maturing of whisky for the desirable ten or fifteen years is an expensive business, as it means a lot of capital lying idle, and at the end the less informed public is not prepared to pay the increased price.

The great temptation is therefore to market blends of cheap grain whisky flavoured slightly with very young malt whisky. Blends with less than 20 per cent malt are known.

The whole situation has become aggravated by taxation, which has now become so great that home consumption is falling and the lesser blenders produce increasingly with an eye on the American market, the more so as they are encouraged to export.

At the moment the market appears to be able to absorb almost unlimited amounts of anything called genuine Scotch whisky because of the way whisky is commonly disguised by other flavours. Already several countries are producing varieties of whisky good enough for the 'whisky cocktail', but this phase will pass as truly as the gin cocktail of the 1920's and we must remember that much big business is not interested in the future of Scotch whisky but in the selling of alcohol. Sir Robert Bruce

Lockhart has already given the warning and it must be repeated here.

A little time ago I was in the lounge of a Highland hotel where to my astonishment lemonade was supplied free to each table. Eventually I dared to ask an old Highlander why he put lemonade in his whisky, a well-known 'first-class blend'. His reply was immediate and definite. 'Ach noo-a-days the whusky haes nae taste.' A true but sad story for the future of whisky.

It is only by keeping up the quality of Scotch whisky that it can maintain its unique position, and in this it is the blenders who have the greatest responsibility.

> There is hardly anything in the world that some man cannot make a little worse and sell a little cheaper, and some people who consider price only are that man's lawful prey (John Ruskin.* 1819–1900).

*John Ruskin, the famous artist and writer, was the son of a wine merchant.

APPENDIX

The Economics of Whisky

by I. A. Glen

The Scotch whisky industry encounters peculiar financial problems because of the prolonged gap between the production and consumption of its product. Apart from oil refining, the industry is notable for employing less labour per £ of commodity made than any other in Britain.

Holding stocks of whisky involves investment over a period of three or more years, and firms which plan to lay down stocks are thus compelled to make forward estimates of markets several years ahead; indeed, in 1970 firms were arranging purchases of new whiskies to be distilled in the autumn of 1975 for bottling perhaps five or more years later. Consequently, whisky business has to be closely attuned to markets, watching current performance and estimating requirements of new whiskies or 'fillings' for future use. The entire Scotch whisky industry has invested in a continued growth in demand by allowing stocks to approach the record level of some 750 million proof gallons.

Distilling and blending are often performed by the same firm, but for purposes of analysis, these functions will be discussed separately. Blenders are mainly concerned with the financing of stocks of Scotch whisky, which appreciate in value as they mature—especially after three years have passed, because the spirit may then be legally consumed in the United Kingdom, and in many other countries. A first-class Highland malt whisky, for example, may treble in value in that time, whereas some other whiskies, less in demand for blending, do not show comparable gains.

On the other hand, distillers do not customarily finance holdings of Scotch whisky, unless they choose to own some stocks as an investment. The distilling side is mostly occupied with the purchase of raw materials, the payment of employees, and the upkeep of plant. An order book is prepared each season. Clients arrange to buy new whisky 'fillings' and they are expected to provide casks, and to pay for their whisky within thirty days of its being distilled. The stocks generally lie in bonded warehouses at their distilleries of origin until required, because whisky matures best in its native environment. Meanwhile, blenders are continually selling whisky, either bottled or in bulk, and they thus renew their supplies of funds to re-invest in stocks.

The profit levels on matured whisky during the 1950's were unusually high, owing to the lack of production during the second world war and the immediate post-war years, with the resulting scarcity of adequately aged holdings. Although profit margins have declined, whisky is still a good investment. Accordingly, speculators outside the regular industry have been buying up about 1½ per cent of the annual output of Scotch whisky, with the intention of selling it at a substantial profit. Distillers of repute try to forestall this type of activity, by dealing only with firms of proven worth, who maintain the quality and good name of Scotch whisky at all times.

Whisky brokerage is an integral part of the Scotch whisky industry, and brokers in whisky fulfil a similar function to brokers on any stock market. There are two aspects to their work; firstly, they hold stocks of 'Scotch', channelling it from distillers to blenders, and secondly, they also have a speculative impact on dealings in whisky.

The whisky boom of recent years has created a need for whisky stocks out of relation to current levels of consumption. Output has been running well in excess of present demands, but so far as brokers are concerned, the favourable pattern of total world consumption has been confirmed in the past, and thus the cost of investing in whisky has been justified. Some firms only have recourse to the open market when their estimates are out of line, as when a particular type of whisky is in short supply, and stocks from brokers must be fed into the pipeline in the blending and bottling plants.

As over 84 per cent of the Scotch whisky sold each year is now consumed in foreign markets, the financing of Scotch whisky for export is a dominant theme in the industry. It is shipped on board duty free, and like many other commodities, whisky is sold 'cash against documents'. This means that the overseas buyer has first to establish a credit in a bank in his own country, and the whisky exporter has to finance the consignment. In the interval, the bank, or its agents, issues to the seller of the whisky a 'letter of credit': this states that the agents will accept a bill of exchange drawn on them by the whisky exporter, who can then have the bill 'discounted', i.e. obtain his money, and the overseas buyer has to put his bank in funds to meet the debt.

There are other methods of financing whisky sales abroad, but much depends upon mutual confidence and trading contacts built up over the years. A risk to which foreign trade in Scotch whisky, or indeed any kind of export, is liable is that of bad debts. Firms have therefore to rely on the services of organisations like the Export Credits Guarantee Department to protect themselves against mishap. The Scotch Whisky Association also provides information to member firms on the state of markets, and the trading prospects therein.

There are of course other facets to investment than stockholding, and the purchase of new fillings, with their problems of warehousing and insurance. Since 1954, there has been a massive expansion in the Scotch whisky industry, causing a doubling in the capacity of most distilleries, in new construction, and in the modernisation of old premises. One malt whisky distillery has raised its output from under 4,000 gallons per week in 1950 to 40,000 gallons per week in 1970, while its warehouses hold over 1 million proof gallons of Scotch whisky—a volume which is now typical of many malt whisky distilleries' bonded stores. Some companies have raised funds on the stock market, some have drawn upon their own private resources, and others have made links with American or Canadian interests, in order to carry out large-scale investment, while Government assistance has been forthcoming to help several firms expand in development areas in Scotland. About a dozen new distilleries have been erected since 1950, three of these having patent stills. A major change has thus overtaken the Scotch whisky industry since the 1930's, when due to slump conditions, exacerbated by Prohibition in the United States, the number of distilleries in production was less than twenty. The industry is now enjoying a period of marked prosperity, having overcome its post-war difficulties of a scarcity of matured stocks, because virtually no whisky had been made between 1942–4 during the second world war.

Scotch whisky is therefore a major growth industry in Scotland, being reckoned to contribute no less than 25 per cent by value to Scottish export earnings each year, and moreover it raises about £198 million in annual revenue for the British Exchequer from home market sales.

Distilling. Costs in the industry are complicated by the fact that manufacture and marketing are often carried out by one enterprise, thus concealing the point that distilling and blending costs may be very different. In common with other British industries, increasing expenditure has been experienced in whisky production in recent years. The filling prices for new whisky have to take account of 33 per cent increases for grain and fuels and 25 per cent increases for transport and labour costs over 1970 costs of production. The main raw material needed for distilling is barley—the cost of which, if home grown, has risen five times since 1939. The industry requires 500,000 tons of barley each season, of which 75 per cent is British grown. One bushel of malting barley, costing say £40 per ton, should be capable of yielding 2·8 gallons of proof spirit, or 24 bottles of malt whisky at 70° proof, retailing at £2·92½ each, allowance having been made for evaporation losses.

In malt whisky production, over 50 per cent of the cost may be attributed to malting barley, 16 per cent to labour, 12 per cent to fuels, and the remainder to other costs such as transport. Many malt whiskies of repute carry a substantial quality premium, because they are so much in demand for blending. It is interesting to find in some distilleries that the cost of fuels has tended to decline relative to other charges, where a change-over from coal to oil-fired boilers for stills has occurred. Some income is earned from the sale of draff, or spent grain, and from feeding stuffs, derived from processed waste liquids, but this activity is not lucrative.

With regard to transport costs, new bulk carriage arrangements have been developed in association with British Rail, whereby grain and fuel is taken to a central depot at Burghead, on the Moray coast, for redistribution to Speyside and other distilleries. A further step is the use of rail-borne whisky tankers; while whisky must be matured in wood, it need not be transported in cask, and considerable savings are effected by moving it in bulk from Highland distilleries to Lowland blending halls. Although these developments have continued, there has been a marked decline in the use of rail transport. The blenders have either equipped themselves with container and other types of lorry, or employ contractors to go round the distilleries collecting the appropriate quantities and types of whisky which they require for their blends.

By comparison, grain whisky is only about half as expensive to produce as pot still whisky, a fact reflected in its filling price. Over 60 per cent of its cost of production may be ascribed to cereals (1 part malt being used to 4 parts maize), 15 per cent to fuels, 10 per cent to labour, and the rest to other costs and overheads. What it gains in economy it loses in character. A few grain whisky distilleries sell carbon dioxide to the aerated water industry, and dispose of a variety of other by-products, such as spent grains and fusel oil.

Distilling in particular is a good example of a capital intensive industry, and the widespread use of automatic systems (e.g. in malting, and in firing stills), is reinforcing this tendency.

While production is rising yearly, employment cannot thus be expected to show a similar growth. It has to be noted that the initial capital investment required to erect a patent still distillery is at least three times as great as for a pot still establishment, and the former can produce more whisky in a month than the latter does in a year. Grain whiskies are the output of a mass production technique using a continuous process, while malt whiskies are essentially craft products, twice or even thrice distilled.

Blending. When the price of a standard bottle of blended Scotch whisky is examined over 70 per cent of the purchase price is duty. The whisky in the bottle constitutes some 3 per cent of the total; bottling adds perhaps another 3 per cent, while the blenders' selling costs and profit margin make up a further 5 per cent of the price. It may be surprising that stock finance (insurance, warehousing and transport charges) for, say, five years, only accounts for 1·5 per cent of the outlay, but this amount increases the longer the whisky is matured. Bottling, packaging, and marketing contribute much more to the blenders' cost pattern, because these aspects have the greatest labour cost content.

Distilling and blending are traditional occupations for men to follow, whereas the bottling of whisky is almost entirely the prerogative of women and girls. Probably fewer than 5,000 persons are engaged in distilling whisky in Scotland, but nearly twice that number are employed in the finishing processes. Although the Scotch whisky industry has a small labour force, it forms a vital element of industrial employment, particularly in the Highlands, and encourages the growth of many ancillary services (e.g. maintenance and transport). Among large British firms, The Distillers Company ranks third in performance in terms of yield of net profit per employee: it is likely that lesser firms whose interests are solely in Scotch whisky earn considerably more profit per employee.

During distilling and subsequent phases in production, the question of duty does not arise, as stocks are stored under bond, in the control of the Customs and Excise authorities. Working capital is thus not tied up in financing this levy, which is passed on to the customer.

Blending firms tend to earn a bigger profit margin on export sales than in the British market, a factor which gives further encouragement to the export bias of the industry. Overseas, 'Scotch' is frequently more expensive than local whiskies, or other comparable spirits; yet its higher price may be associated with status and social prestige, especially in sophisticated markets, such as the United States of America. The growing volume of bulk exports to that country has given cause for disquiet in the industry. Leading proprietary blends have had to enter the bulk export business (which is favoured by U.S. tariff legislation) because they were losing ground to American bottled 'Scotch', which was sold at a much lower price. This development could lead to the decline of bottling, until the point where this branch of the industry caters solely for the home market. Anxiety is also felt about the volume of immature whisky which is being exported, and which could do irreparable harm to the reputation and high standing of all Scotch whiskies.

In Britain, Scotch whisky has no price advantage over other spirits and the market is not a dynamic one, home consumption representing a decreasing share of total world demand. Until March 1965, resale price maintenance was operated, and prices were 'recommended' for use at home and abroad. The passing of the Resale Prices Act (1964) did not justify firms in pursuing claims for exemption from the provisions regarding price fixing. Accordingly, when The Distillers Company announced that it would take no further action (and in so doing effectively abandoned price agreements), other firms had little alternative but to follow their leader. Notwithstanding, competition is keen in the industry, it shows itself in a commercial 'gamesmanship'—to market better whiskies, to devise new advertising methods, to provide more efficient sales and service facilities.

Competition takes many forms, but until the abolition of R.P.M., price cuts were normally excluded, the argument being that there was little room for reducing retail prices when tax formed the preponderant portion of the final price. With the cessation of price agreements, however, many standard blends were reduced in price. The assumption was that a larger turnover would offset the small margin (about 1p per bottle) left to the distributor. Since 1966, the duty has been increased by £0·32½ per bottle, and this has been handed on to the public. Soaring costs, the result of increasing costs of production and wage–price inflation have forced firms to raise their prices for standard blends, to as much as £2·92½ per bottle, but some retail outlets have blends available at £2·50 per bottle. It is cold comfort to point out to the consumer that the actual Scotch in his bottle only accounts for some 3 per cent of the sum he has paid for it.

APPENDIX

The Larger Distillery Groups

THE DISTILLERS COMPANY

Aberfeldy, Aultmore, Balmenach, Banff, Benrinnes, Benromach, Brackla, Brechin (North Port), Brora, Caledonian, Cambus, Cameron Bridge, Caol Ila, Cardow, Carsebridge, Clynelish, Coleburn, Convalmore, Cragganmore, Craigllachie, Dailuaine, Dallas Dhu, Dalwhinnie, Glendullan, Glen Elgin, Glenkinchie, Glenlochy, Glenlossie, Glentauchers, Glenury, Hillside, Imperial, Knockdhu, Lagavulin, Linkwood, Linlithgow (St Magdalene), Lochnagar, Millburn, Mortlach, Oban, Ord, Port Dundas, Port Ellen, Rosebank, Speyburn, Talisker, Teaninich, Mannochmore, Glen Mohr, Glen Albyn.

A. BELL

Blair Athol, Dufftown, Inchgower.

GLEN GRANT-GLENLIVET

Glenlivet, Glen Grant, Longmorn.

W. GRANT

Glenfiddich, Balvenie, Girvan, Ladybank.

HIGHLAND DISTILLERS

Highland Park, Tamdhu, Glenglassaugh, Glen Rothes, Bunnahabain, Glengoyne.

INTERNATIONAL DISTILLERS & VINTNERS

Glenspey, Strathmill, Knockando, Ardroich.

INVERGORDON

Invergordon, Ben Wyvis, Tamintoul, Deanston, Tullibardine, Bruichladdich, Bladnoch.

SCOTTISH & NEWCASTLE BREWERIES

Jura, Glenallachie.

LONG JOHN INTERNATIONAL

Tormore, Laphroaig, Glenugie, Ben Nevis, Strathclyde (with grain).

SEAGRAM

Strathisla, Glenkeith.

TEACHERS

Glendronach, Ardmore.

HIRAM WALKER

Dumbarton, Inverleven, Glenburgie, Milton Duff, Pulteney, Balblair, Scapa, Glencadam.

SUPPLEMENT

Aberlour—Glenlivet

Until 1973 this whisky was almost entirely exported by its owners, the White Heather Distillers of Glasgow. The distillery where it is made is on the main road to the south of the town of Aberlour where it is tucked into a steep little valley which the River Lour has carved out on its way to the Spey. Its water arises from the side of Ben Rinnes which dominates the whole area and supplies water to many nearby distilleries. In the distillery area itself is the Well of St. Drostan, an Englishman and patron saint of Aberlour, who was a missionary in these parts who became Archbishop of Canterbury in A.D. 959. He was later canonised as St. Dunstan. Originally there were mills in the valley but there has been a distillery here since 1826. It was rebuilt in 1879 after a fire and since had several owners, amongst whom was Holt of Manchester who bought it in 1920 and produced Holt's Mountain Cream. Holt in 1945 sold it to Campbell who have now had it for four generations and who have bonding warehouses and a cooperage in Glasgow. It is one of the tidiest and best kept distilleries I know.

The whisky is smooth, round and has a distinctive flavour and is said to owe its characteristics to the use of barley which is "not fat but with high protein" and its water made famous by St. Drostan ten centuries ago. It is not without interest that the new nearby distillery Tamnavoulin prides itself on its whisky being made from a "plump" barley. This is not so smooth or flavoursome, but it may become so as it gets older.

Amalgamated Distilled Products

This company has recently become quoted on the London Stock Exchange as based on Kingsborne Distillers, Thomas Shaw and A. Gilles of Glasgow. They own Glen Scotia Distillery in Campbeltown and the Grangemouth Bonding Company where their products are blended and bottled. The old distillery in Campbeltown has recently been reconstructed and doubled in size.

In addition to Glen Scotia which has already been described (page 41) the company produces Old Court for export and Royal Culross, named after the old seventeenth-century village on the other side of the Firth of Forth. This is in the very first class of blends with a rich flavour which obviously comes from well matured malts. There could be no better advertisement for a new company.

Glendeveron

This excellent malt is made in Macduff Distillery near the small town of that name and draws its water from the River Deveron. The distillery which is a very modern cement structure was built by Brodie Hepburn in 1960 but was sold to Block, Grey & Block, the whisky exporters in London. In 1972 it was sold again to William Lawson of Coatbridge. Lawsons was originally a wine and spirit merchant in Dundee. Glendeveron was off the market for a short time but I understand is returning.

The main blend of the firm which is largely exported is William Lawson's Blended Scotch Whisky but there is a subsidiary company Clan Munroe Whisky Ltd. which exports a brand called King Edward I. Such are the complications of the whisky trade!

Glendullan

Another famous distillery of Dufftown. It was built in 1840 for William Williams of Aberdeen but after the First World War this company was merged with Alexander & Macdonald of Leith and the old firm of Greenlees Brothers (1840) of London and Glasgow under the title of Macdonald, Greenlees & Williams which joined the Distillers Company in 1926 as Macdonald Greenlees.

Glendullan only became available as a single malt in 1972.

It is indeed a really grand whisky, robust and full of character and flavour, but mellow. Naturally it is the basis of the well-known blends of Macdonald & Greenlees, President, Sandy Macdonald and the famous Old Parr. Mr. Parr was an old farmer, on the estates of the Earl of Arundel near Shrewsbury, who became famous for his virility. He fathered a child at the age of 105 and became such a celebrity and personality that he was brought to court by the Earl, painted by Rubens and Van Dyck and in due course, when the high life of London led to his decease at the age of 152, was at the instigation of Charles I buried in Westminster Abbey amongst the poets. Apart from his tablet on the floor of the Abbey his name lives on in the noble blend which in fact was invented many years later. Its popularity especially in Japan shows what a good name can do when the whisky is also good.

In 1972 there was added nearby in the same Fiddich Valley the greatest of all modern distilleries with stills holding seven thousand gallons, indeed one of the great sights of the world of whisky. We can only hope that the new stills will provide whiskies as good as the old.

GLENTURRET

A small distillery in a beautiful little glen of the River Turret which runs from Loch Turret in the hills between Crief and Comrie in Stirlingshire. The parish records show that whisky was made here in 1775 but like so many small distilleries it fell on evil days until it was rebuilt by Thomas Stewart. It was refurbished again by the enthusiastic Mr. James Fawlie in 1960 who installed a completely new plant and in the last ten years its production has been increased fourfold.

The whisky, which has a somewhat flowery flavour, a little reminiscent of Glenmorangie, won the silver seal at the International Wine and Spirit Competition in London in 1972. This competition is sponsored by the Club Oenoligigue which has a very distinguished and knowledgeable patronage. When it is good it is very good.

Inver House

This unusual distillery to the south of Airdrie is new to the world of whisky in many ways, having been built by Publicker Industries Incorporated of Philadelphia, U.S.A. It doesn't look like a distillery at all but it is a very efficient place. It has no pagoda topped kiln and much of its apparatus, even some of the wash backs, are out of doors, but of course they have lids. The distillery complex is on a rugged site of 300 acres where the old Moffat paper mill used to be.

Malt is made in huge quantities sufficient to supply other distilleries. This is done by the German Wanderhaufen method in which the steeped barley is germinated in huge saladin-like tanks while being aerated by large corkscrew-like screws. This malt is subsequently dried and peated by forcing hot peated air through it. A large amount of labour is thereby saved.

Both malt and grain whiskies are made by the classical methods of the pot still and the patent still and their products are excellent. Its malt is Glen Flagler, of the classical type with no special feature.

In 1973 the company acquired Bladnock distillery which makes an excellent Lowland malt which improves greatly as it matures (see page 35).

Its popular blends are Inver House and MacArthur, the latter a name taken over from an old Inverness company (1877). The popularity of the latter is increased by its cheapness compared with many blends but it is a pleasant whisky with a distinctive flavour. A really de luxe blend is also made, Pinwinnie, called after a nearby farm, which is certainly one of the best blends made. Its rich flavour shows that the blender really knows how to select his malts, but it is naturally very expensive.

With all these pleasant products and so much room for expansion, the company has a great future.

Invergordon Holdings

Invergordon Distillery was the first of this increasing group, and is on a delightful site overlooking the Cromarty Firth, one of the great homes of the British Fleet in time of war but after the war under the inspiration of Provost Grigor of Inverness a distillery was erected to give employment to men who had become redundant. It is however no ordinary distillery. It is really a great factory capable of making annually ten million gallons of grain whisky by the patent-still method. Actually it was begun by a group of men, many of whom had little experience of making whisky at all, but they were enthusiastic and succeeded in making such a good whisky so cheaply that they became almost unpopular in the trade. Fortunately the first manager, Frank Thomson, a local accountant, had already enlisted the financial support of London Merchant Securities which saw the future of the project. A malt whisky distillery known as Ben Wyvis was added on the same site while another new distillery Tamnavoulin-Glenlivet was built in 1966 in the famous Glenlivet valley and here it must be said that this new concrete building looks strangely out of place in such a highland scene. No doubt it will, like its famous and inelegant neighbour opposite, the Glenlivet Distillery, mellow with age—the whisky too will improve greatly as it matures.

Bruichladdich Distillery in the Island of Islay was purchased and, later in 1972, two other distilleries—Tullibardine and Deanston. Tullibardine, in the small town of Blackford, was originally a brewery but since 1949 it has made a malt whisky with a quite outstanding almost wine-like flavour, but it is in short supply and alas, it is no longer issued at 80°.

Deanston was originally a textile mill with an ample supply of electricity made from the Teith, a tributary of the Forth.

Thus it is seen that with such a plentiful supply of grain whisky and such a variety of malts Invergordon is well placed to produce really excellent blends. This is marketed as Findlaters Finest Old Scotch Whisky. William Findlater began some business in 1823 and is now associated with Mackie, Todd & Co. Invergordon also makes for Findlater a vatted malt called Mar Lodge named after the highland residence of a Princess Royal near Balmoral. It also produces a new vatted malt, Old Bannockburn, which was the name previously used by Deanston Mill. In addition, it produces Longmans, Glen Eagle and a twelve-year-old De Luxe blend, Glenfoyle.

The Vatted Malts

Vatted malts are mixtures of malts or blends without any grain whisky being added. For the most part they are gimmicks made to satisfy the demand for more flavoured whiskies and of course at a considerably higher price than most blends. Somehow most miss the boat in the sense that they prove how really skilled blending is. We read of William Sanderson trying a hundred blends before he got Vat 69. I am afraid too that many contain immature whiskies. Some are quite smooth but somehow the mixture of flavours is wrong, as if one took a mixture of different kinds of chocolate into the mouth at the same time. The result would be an indeterminate taste. It has become almost a fashion for wine merchants, some of great respectability, to produce pure vatted malt, but the only one I know which has really succeeded is Strathconon—a product of James Buchanan, the maker of Black & White. Others are by Berry's (All malt), Findlaters (Old Mar), Haig (Glen Leven) and Harrods.

Bibliography

ALLEN, H. WARNER, 1950. *No. 3 St James's Street*, Chatto & Windus, London.

BARNARD, A., 1887. *The Whisky Distilleries of the United Kingdom*, Harper, 1887; reprinted 1969 by David & Charles, Newton Abbot.

BIRNIE, WILLIAM, 1937 and 1964. *The Distillation of Highland Malt Whisky*, Private.

DAICHES, D., 1969. *Scotch Whisky*, Deutsch.

DISTILLERS COMPANY LTD, 1966. *D.C.L. and Scotch Whisky*.

DUNNET, ALASTAIR, 1953. *The Land of Scotch*, The Scotch Whisky Association.

FORBES, K. J., 1948. *A Short History of the Art of Distillation*, Brill, Leiden.

GLENFARCLAS, *The Scotsman*, 27 October 1927.

GLEN GRANT, *The Scotsman*, 28 August 1967.

GLENLIVET (1924 reprinted 1959). *The Annals of the Distillery*.

GUNN, NEIL, 1935. *Whisky and Scotland*, Routledge, London.

LAVER, JAMES, 1958. *The House of Haig*, John Haig & Co. Ltd.

LOCKHART, R. BRUCE, 1959, 1967. *Scotch*, Putnam, London.

MACDONALD, AENEAS, 1930. *Whisky*, The Porpoise Press, Edinburgh.

ROSS, JAMES, 1970, *Whisky*, Routledge & Kegan Paul, London.

THE SCOTCH WHISKY ASSOCIATION, 1957. *Scotch Whisky, Questions & Answers*.

SILLETT, S. W., 1965. *Illicit Scotch*, Beaver Books, Aberdeen.

'Teachers', *The Times*, 22 March 1962.

WHEATLEY, DENNIS, 1965. *The Eight Ages of Justerini's*.

WILSON, ROSS, 1959. *Scotch Made Easy*, Hutchinson, London.

WILSON, ROSS, 1963. *The House of Sanderson*, William Sanderson.

WILSON, ROSS, 1962 onwards. 'Scotch Whisky Distillers of Today', and 'Seventy years of the Scotch Whisky Industry', two series of articles in the *Wine & Spirit Trade Record*.

WILSON, ROSS, 1973. *Scotch, its History and Romance*.

WRIGHT, HEDLEY, 1963. 'A note on Campbeltown & the Distilling Trade', *Wine & Spirit Trade Record*.

In addition, almost all companies have been good enough to send me booklets or information on their history.

Index

Index

Index